Searching for Osiris

&

The Tree of Life

Searching for Osiris, RN Vooght

By

RN Vooght

Searching for Osiris, RN Vooght

Acknowledgement:

The Myth of Osiris is essentially typified as a Hero's Journey. There is no other Hero held in higher esteem than that of my own father. This one's for you dad.

My Hero.

Searching for Osiris, RN Vooght

CONTENTS

SEARCHING FOR OSIRIS

Myth: *A traditional story, especially one concerning the early history of a people or explaining a natural or social phenomenon, typically involving supernatural beings or events.*

Legend has it that there was a so-called 'mythological' landmass known as *Atlantis* which disappeared beneath the waves 12,000 years Before Present. This otherwise metaphorical mystery has almost become completely erased from living memory. *Atlantis*, it is said, was home to a highly sophisticated and spiritually adept pre-diluvian seafaring civilization. This accomplished society of master stone masons were capable of traversing and mapping a wholly interconnected globe – the fingerprints of which appear to weave together not only a map of unimaginable megalithic wonder but also, a map of the human mind and beyond. And regardless of our religious leanings in the modern era, our ancestors appear to have succeeded in maintaining a myth-illogical template of humanity's hidden higher self and chiselled it into stone. Plato's tale describing the disappearance of said civilization around 9,700 BC had largely been dismissed by the mainstream. Until now, the notion of a long-lost pre-flood civilization had been rendered almost impossible due to the archaeological evidence lacking between the rise of said sea levels and the accepted chronology of civilized high society around 3100 BC. The evidence, however, does exist and lies in ancient Anatolia, modern-day Turkey. Gobekli Tepe is a vast and cosmologically aligned temple complex that still remains less than five percent excavated. Dated to around 12,000

1

years BP, the complex displays a plethora of intricate high-relief pillar carvings that may encode an ancient cataclysm that disrupted the course and subsequent rise of humanity. This profoundly revealing methodology wasn't even considered possible for another 6000 years, but the fact remains, it's there. And the facts have changed according to the resulting research therein.

Furthermore, we also witness a vast and ever-expanding number of unexplainable and logic-defying construction techniques and commonalities spanning continents that are classically theorized as being independent of each other. Even more astounding, however, they also share and wholly reflect the same cosmological ideology regarding the otherwise mythological *Tree of Life* – the roots of which appear to span both time and inner space. With this in mind, is it beyond the realms of plausible rationality to suggest that the post-flood survivors fled the fallout of the Americas and rebuilt a culture from an already established technological know-how that has since been otherwise mis-accredited to an Ancient Egyptian society that seemingly sprang from nothing and erected structures which witnessed an inexplicable and thus illogical decline in craftsmanship thereafter?

Almost every ancient civilization, including those who inhabited some of the most remote and isolated corners of the planet, all recall a time whereby the so-called *Gods* kick-started and thus reseeded a devasted populous with the knowledge and tools to overcome the catastrophic fallout of the end of the last Ice Age. But who, or indeed what, were these Gods? Where did they come from? Where did they go? Will they return? Or rather, did they ever really leave us?

IT'S WRITTEN IN THE STARS

Ancient Egyptian mythology is steeped in tradition; a tradition whereby Egyptologists prefer to remain ostensibly steadfast in defending an outdated paradigm that has lacked the courage and conviction to keep up with the science which once supported it. Are we really to believe that a technologically evolved civilization capable of constructing an unparalleled colossus such as the Great Pyramid, was also a society that endeavoured to preach that their anthropomorphic and deified creations were anything more or less than the allegorical archetypes to which they clearly allude to? Either, the Ancient Egyptians quarried, cut, and placed over two million cumbersome blocks of limestone and granite in the name of a real-life ram-headed creator God intending it to house and commemorate the body of a dead pharaoh, an absurdity in the extreme, or they inherited a wealth of accumulated understanding from a far older ancestral lineage to which they readily accept and refer to. For the Ancient Egyptians, themselves refer to a civilized timeline in excess of 36,000 years, to which they fondly recall Zep Tepe or the 'First Time'. And it's not just Ancient Egypt. There appears to be a plethora of ancient civilizations such as the Mayans, Inca, Aztecs, Aboriginals, Greeks, and Norse Scandinavians who all share the same mythological cosmology which encapsulates a template for Gods of Resurrection, third eye symbology, and the so-called Tree of Life. It is my intention to look at these mythologies through more of a scientific lens and focus upon both the megaliths and the molecules which I believe play a crucial part in the way we perceive the human story, and indeed, reality! Whether we're conscious of it or not, the natural phenomenon that is N, N dimethyltryptamine, was and still is key to understanding the riddle of human consciousness. N, N dimethyltryptamine, also known as DMT, is a psychedelic chemical compound that permeates the natural world. This Class A hallucinogen can be found within almost all plant-based life and throughout the animal kingdom; we find it inside the human brain, lungs, eyes, and cerebrospinal fluid, yet even more bizarrely; no one knows why! DMT or the *Spirit Molecule*, the name it rather aptly adopted after human trials were undergone by a group of volunteers enlisted by Dr. Rick Strassman, an American clinical associate professor of psychiatry at the University of New Mexico School of Medicine, USA. As it appears to induce a hyper-vivid and geometrically profound 'Out of Body Experience' which establishes the practitioner's belief in an otherworldly dimension or reality beyond the scope of our uninitiated sensory environment. Described as an entheogen – a compound word meaning 'god within', DMT has been used as a tool to elevate human consciousness by indigenous tribespeople for thousands of years. It's the active component of the South American shamanic brew known as Ayahuasca; which means *Vine of the Soul*. Classical case reports uncover an intriguing if not profound insight into this wholly-otherworldly mindscape. Typical 'breakthrough' experiences frequently involve encounters with benevolent angel-like beings and superiorly intellectual entities within the framework of an impossibly hyperdimensional and alien reality.

It is largely accepted that the DMT experience is likened to a mini-death, whereby the initiates ego or soul is temporarily dissolved into an infinite entity-rich source of pure and interconnected understanding before returning blissfully and metaphorically *resurrected* just as Jesus was said to have done around two thousand years ago. Here then, I hope to continue the search for Osiris; an allegorical human truth whom I believe is linked directly to the notion of a long-lost and spiritually-adept civilization who understood the nature of both the human mind and the planet and its vital role in elevating human consciousness beyond the scope of which we claim to understand in the modern era.

Imagine, if you will, that here in the 21st century where we stand upon the cusp of sending someone to the moon once again – Mars even, yet we still have almost absolutely no idea what happens to the conscious mind after death! Zero. The riddle of human consciousness and the nature of the mind is the greatest riddle of all. So, here we stand with the advent of space exploration, yet we find ourselves poking around somewhat blindly seeking the answers to life's biggest questions; who are we? How did we get here? And of course, what's next? But what if we're not 'the greatest' after all? Yes, outer space is certainly worthwhile probing but what if it's inner space where the answers to such fundamentally profound, albeit tantalizingly taboo questions do indeed lie? Furthermore, is it beyond the realms of plausible rational to suggest that someone, somewhere had in fact worked it all out and inserted a scientifically viable explanation to who, or indeed what we are, into the zeitgeist of an otherwise interconnected global society lost to the historical narrative for the benefit of future generations of humanity? Classically speaking, the dawn of civilized society emerged from the nomadic plains of the hunter-gather mindset some 5000 years or so ago; but it wasn't until the advent of electricity some 150 years ago that we were still sitting by candlelight and were in relative darkness until the meteoric strides that technological knowhow has thrust upon humankind's otherwise unextraordinary outlook! Now, anatomically correct human beings like you and me have roamed the Earth for at least the last 300,000 years. Think about that for a moment. 300,000 years. 5,000 of which is accountable for the entire chronological catalogue of human history! What about the other 295,000 years? Where's the rest? Before the discovery of

Gobekli Tepe in Ancient Anatolia, modern-day Turkey, mainstream archaeology insisted that nothing, absolutely nothing came before the agriculturally astute Ancient Egyptians and Sumerian civilizations which appeared to arise almost spontaneously with the tools necessary to kickstart society along with the written word. Now, however, our ancient artisans of prehistoric Mesopotamia appear to have been quite the architects; architects who were able enough to erect constructions on such a scale beyond that which was otherwise scoffed at by modern-day historians and academia who now accept that the dating of civilized society does, in fact, to go back at least 12,000 years ago! And who knows how far beyond that?

Moreover, it's not necessarily just the architectural prowess of their construction techniques that has made the so-called neigh-sayers sit up a little straighter a pay more attention. Indeed, it's the ever-present animal iconography of the era which is seemingly far too readily accepted as baring cosmologically akin towards fertility symbology instead of reading into its all too apparent assertion towards brain anatomy and the house of human consciousness! Ancient art transcends language and there are many arte-facts for us to reconsider!

For example, Ancient Greek mythology appears to hold a far deeper and more underlying scientific meaning than anyone first thought possible in the modern era. Take the myth of Pegasus. At first glance, the much-fabled flying horse born of a union between Medusa and Poseidon takes flight after the beheading of his mother at the hands of Perseus. Yet because of the nature of Poseidon being a God of the Sea, and indeed horses, should we be led to believe that Pegasus may, in fact, be a seahorse? Absolutely!

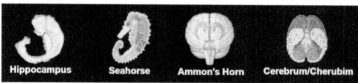

Hippocampus   Seahorse   Ammon's Horn   Cerebrum/Cherubim

A seahorse who was favoured by the Goddess, Mnemosyne – the Goddess of Memory. However, seahorses can't fly; so, what does this really tell us? We know that Pegasus is white and for all intents and purposes has wings, but clearly, this doesn't make much sense – that is unless we decide to look at it through a wholly scientific lens. The

Pes Hippocampus

word seahorse arrives via the Ancient Greeks and translates as the *hippocampus*, and for good reason too. The hippocampus of the human brain is a white eminence responsible for higher brain functions such as memory recall and is shaped like its namesake – a seahorse! Further to the mythology, however, Pegasus was favoured by the Goddess of Memory after his hoof was said to have struck the fountain of Hippocrene on Mount Helicon which caused its waters, or indeed, memory to flow. But here's the kicker, quite literally. There's a part of the hippocampus called the *Pes Hippocampus* which is shaped rather explicitly like a creature's paw or hoof! Moreover, the otherwise missing wings of our fabled flying seahorse take the shape of the brain's cerebrum; another Ancient Greek word whose etymology is closely associated with the biblical winged cherubim! Should it surprise us then to find the same meticulous methodology being incorporated into Renaissance Period art also? Michelangelo's much-famed fresco which adorns the vaulted ceiling of the Vatican, in Rome, is one of sheer wonder.

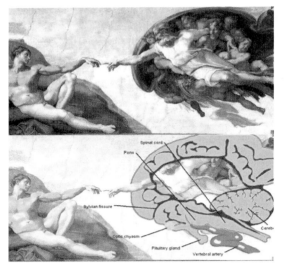

However, this 1512 masterpiece, *The Creation of Adam,* depicts God giving the essence of life to His creation; but this particular rendition is one which not only appears to give the breath of life but does, in fact, snatch it from within the beholder also! Quite how this didactic treasure has been overlooked for so long almost beggar's belief!

On the 10th of October 1990, an article discussing the aforementioned fresco appeared in The New York Times. Practiced physician Dr. Frank Lynn Meshberger, proposed that Michelangelo had not only created a mindbogglingly complex work of art, but he'd rather purposefully exposed the anatomy of the human mind also! What Meshberger suggested was, that the billowing cloud formations and fluttering robes of the Lord, were not merely so. Said clouds and garments were indeed more descriptive of human brain anatomy including the medulla, optic chasm, pituitary gland, and spinal cord which had gone quite blissfully unnoticed for almost 500 years. The painting was thus depicting an allegorical blueprint of the biomechanics of the house of human consciousness. A divine spark indeed!

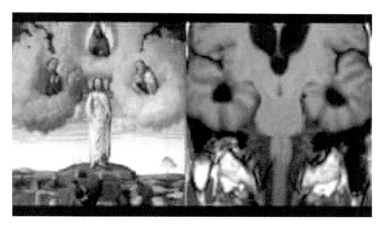

Furthermore, Michelangelo was by no means alone when artfully placing answers to the nature of the mind onto ceilings and canvases alike. Seventeen years after Meshberger's divine revelation, respected neuroscientist Alessandro Paluzzi reminded us of this revolutionary genius of a bygone era. Paluzzi had discovered that Flemish artisan Gerard David's 1520 rendition of *The Transfiguration of Christ into the Light*, was far more descriptive of a segmented human brain. Paluzzi believes that David has clearly and expertly informing us of the importance and functionality of brain anatomy including the hippocampus, ventricles, pineal gland, and brain stem in relation to the riddle of consciousness – or God-like state of mind. How long has this template been used – didactic art describing brain anatomy? Well, for at least the last five hundred years as Michelangelo and co have bear witnessed.

But could it be longer? Much longer!? In 2018 archaeologists discovered several relatively untouched tombs located in Jinan's Jiyang District, China. Dating back to the Han Dynasty (circa. 206 BC-AD 220), the 20 x 15-meter tombs are the largest known of their kind. A great number of porcelains, bones, coins, and pottery were excavated amongst which were elaborately designed high-relief carvings which appeared to depict 'goats' heads.' However, upon closer inspection, these otherwise animalistic artisans may be better described as human brain anatomy also! The ever-present horn-like hippocampus and brain stem's medulla oblongata and pons are anatomically correct to an almost impossible degree! Another enlightening example arrives via the inquisitive mind of researcher Danny Wilton who compares the irrefutable commonalities between the human brain stem alongside the wholly (not be confused with holy) iconic crucified Christ, which are almost as obvious and pain-staking as the cruci-fiction itself! It is also of utmost importance here that we note that the placement of Christ's head is in direct correlation to the pineal gland. Jesus was said to have worn a crown of thorns while being crucified; the significance of which being the crown was said to have been fashioned from the extremely barbed acacia variety to which our

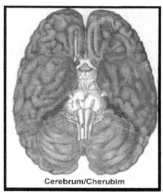

Cerebrum/Cherubim

investigation shall shortly return! We are told that Jesus was said to be crucified in Golgotha. Golgotha is Ancient Aramaic which translates directly as the *skull*, and for all intents and purposes, the bible is extremely explicit when citing that 'Jesus is in You!'. It goes as far as stating that God resides in temples that are built in silence, not of stone, and that is made not by the hands of man; thus, the temples to which it is clearly alluding, are the temples of one's own skull. Look within. Further to this, however, the bible dictates that God dwells between the wings of the cherubim. Ex-pastor and researcher Bill Donahue exposes the etymology of the word cherubim which derives from the Greek word 'cerebrum'. The suffix 'cere' means to cover whereby the job of the brain's cerebrum is to thus cover and protect the brain stem. The Bible further conveys the notion of brain anatomy via quotes such as 'the wings of the cherubim touched to walls of the temple', insomuch that the cerebrum surrounds the brain stem and touches the temples of the skull. And if we were ever in any doubt regarding the profundity of such text, the cerebrum is shaped like the wings of an angel albeit, cherubim! Moreover, this didactic template isn't strictly a Christian conundrum! Hindu ideology also paints a profound picture should we care to look at these ancient artisans as it was surely intended. Not unlike their Ancient Egyptian counterparts, quite remarkable, is the clear and present congruity of the natural configuration of the brain and the Vedic elephant-headed God Ganesha – patron to the sciences, and the deva of intellect and wisdom!

Moreover, this tried and tested template maybe even more archaic still. The artistic characteristics of the Ancient Egyptian dwarf 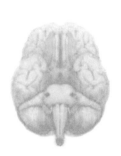 god, Bes, a prominent figure throughout the New Kingdom between 1800 BC – 1100 BC, share a striking similarity to our old friend the hippocampus also. The keen eye of fellow researcher and writer Daniel Moran reveals the incomprehensible commonalities between the over-prominent eye-line of the impish deity and that of Ammon's Horn; another scientific anomaly also known as the hippocampus proper! However, it's certainly not a case of pareidolia or faces in clouds here, because the mythology of Bes, like Osiris as we have already witnessed, is also synonymous

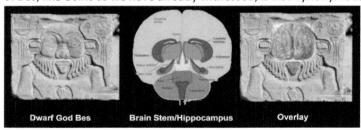

Dwarf God Bes   Brain Stem/Hippocampus   Overlay

with a consciousness-altering analogue which is spoken of in scientific arenas with regard to the psychedelic potential of Peganum Harmala, or Syrian Rue. Syrian Rue is classically identified as a DMT-infused and entheogenic medicine or tool. This Ancient Arabic intoxicant, Harmal (also spelled, Harmel) was also recognized in Ancient Egypt as the 'Plant of Bes'. Throughout Egypt, Bes was commonly associated with being a protector of dreams, which in itself may have been likened to the otherworldly connotations of the dream-like state of expanded consciousness we identify with the DMT experience in the modern era. The entire thought process regarding the ever-present psychedelic compound DMT in Ancient Egypt appears to come full circle once again, as this very same analogue was also recognized as Haoma, the Ancient Iranian elixir of immortality. A 2nd-century initiation inventory refers to the 'noub tree' in context to haoma which may also be likened to the Tree of Life which contained the entire universe under the watchful eye of the Ancient Egyptian deity, Osiris. Osiris, as we discovered is almost indistinguishable from Jesus, the Amen; Amen or Ammon being scientifically exposed as an ancient allegory for Ammon's Horn of the hippocampus!

Jesus/Amen   Amun Ra   Zeus Ammon   Jupiter Ammon   Alexander the Great

Ammon, we find, is also synonymous with Zeus Ammon, the Greek Godhead who like Alexander the Great, was commonly depicted with ram-like horns. Zeus Ammon however, was also akin to the Ancient Egyptian Solar Deity, Amun. Amun himself is synonymous with the sign of the ram no less! Adding further weight to this archaic axiom, we learn that Amun is also described as the Amen; an endearing and biblical term used to describe Jesus, the Lamb of God! Lest we forget, the bible's primary message is that *God is Light*, just as Jesus is described as the *Light of the World*! The Bible rather matter-of-factly states that Jacob witnessed the face of God in a place he called Peniel; and somewhat coincidently, science describes the pineal gland of the human brain as the light receptor of the body!

Matthew 6:22

The light of the body is the eye: If therefore thine eye be single, thy whole body shall be filled with light.

Here then, could there be more to the myths than first meets the eye? The pineal glands' scientific name is the epiphysis cerebri, the etymology of which is directly related to the word epiphany; a moment of divine inspiration emanating from within the midst of one's mind's eye! The pineal gland is described in medical dictionaries the globe over as being pinecone-shaped, but if one were to bisect it, it actually looks like an eye. Furthermore, and rather incredibly, it even has the same rod and cone structure as a normal eye. Even more astonishing is the fact that it is also connected to the optic thalami which almost completely renders it a *third eye*! The now iconic Ancient Egyptian

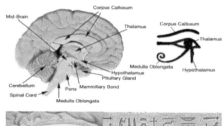

Eye of Horus, also known as the Wedjat talisman offers further insight into this archaic state of mind. This much-famed ancient *all-seeing eye* has more recently been described by the ongoing research of Gary Osborn as correlating directly alongside the brain's thalamus, hypothalamus, corpus callosum, medulla oblongata, and pineal gland.

Classically associated alongside the *wedjat* is a deity central to the Ancient Egyptian pantheon of Gods. Thoth, God of Wisdom, Magic, the Sciences, and Master of Knowledge, we learn, is usually depicted as a baboon. This otherwise perplexing mystery regarding an ancient understanding under the guise of a mischievous monkey makes a world more sense if we decide to break away from the mainstream misgivings and look instead into the deeper metaphorical mindset of the ancients. Thoth or *thought* may be better described as brain anatomy once again. Instead of monkeying around with insane ideologies such as an anthropomorphically-obsessed ancestry who were accomplished enough to construct megalithic colossi such as the Great Pyramid

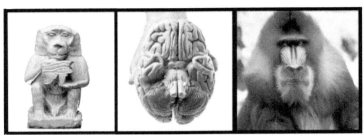

(a feat beyond our own technological ingenuity today), and then deify daft animal-headed anomalies in order to preserve an altogether nonsensical narrative, which is still being peddled and pushed by the paradigm-protecting crackpots incapable of thinking outside of their baboon-brained boxes, which they barricade and bolster by blindfolding themselves *and* those who continue to support them!

It's somewhat unfortunate that those who remain blissfully blinkered and thus blinded by the all too obvious light, appear to be neglecting themselves of a far higher science hidden by the hypocrisy they hold so dear to their hearts. But the writings on the wall – quite literally! Those who have eyes to see, however, are privy to the possibilities presented within a prehistoric picture that paints our ancient ancestry in an altogether alternative worldview. The myth of Osiris arrives via the perfectly preserved pyramid texts which adorn the ceilings and walls of the pyramid of Unas which is dated to around 3100 BC. The etymology of the God of Resurrection tells a story of its own also; '*Os*' has a plethora of meanings including both '*god*' and '*open*'. Indeed, those who have eyes to see do not need a further explanation for the suffix '*iris*'! The word *iris* is Ancient Greek for the word *rainbow*, and by design, if not a cosmic coincidence, the angles of the Great Pyramid of Giza

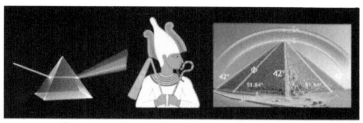

are generally accepted as reflecting an angle of 42 degrees – the precise angle required to perceive a rainbow!

On the face of it, Osiris is an Ancient Egyptian oddity. This green-skinned gatekeeper to the *otherworld* is well worth looking into for several reasons. *Everything* here is allegorical.

Ancient Egyptian mythology reveals rather profound insight into the curious riddle that is human consciousness and is also the earliest reference to the mythological T*ree of Life*. The tale of Osiris begins during an elaborate banquet where the guests had been invited by Seth (or Set depending on your source), who was Osiris's wicked brother, to each lay down inside a beautifully ornate coffer and suggested whoever fitted it comfortably could keep it. Guest after guest tried the magnificent coffer, each struggling with its dimensions and either coming up too short or too tall, until the turn of Osiris. Osiris duly laid down inside to find it fit him perfectly. Yet to the guest's stunned amazement, Seth and his cohorts seized the opportunity and swiftly fastened the coffer with Osiris inside before tossing it into the River Nile. The coffer eventually ran ashore upon the coastal banks of Byblos in modern-day Lebanon, where Osiris became further entombed within the trunk of a resplendent Tamarisk tree. After several years, the King of Byblos ordered the felling of the beautiful tree as it was to be carved into a pillar that would adorn the halls of his grandiose palace. Osiris's sister and consort Isis learned of her lover's fate and bargained with the King who duly agreed to release Osiris from his untimely grave. Seth was enraged by this and disembodied Osiris thus dispatching his brother once and for all. Legend further dictates that Osiris is symbolically associated with the constellation of Orion, a celestial God of Resurrection.

Here then we have a God of Resurrection immortalized on a macrocosmic scale as the constellation of Orion, who is also considered as the complete embodiment of 'all things acacia' – our proverbial Ancient Egyptian Tree of Life. So, what can be said of these otherwise conflicting mythologies? Either our resurrected God resides above us within the cosmos and is depicted as Orion, the celestial hunter of the heavens, or He resides here on Earth as the spiritual essence of the ethnobotanical variety of the acacia. Osiris it transpires, was also likened to the *lifeblood* of the acacia. Now, it is said, 'God is everywhere!' but what does this really tell us? Indeed, what does God look like?

Should we decide to pierce the veil of the dogmatic and materialistic consumer culture that is rife within traditional western society, the somewhat over-cited term *mythological*, tends to lend more than an apparent leaning towards the myth-*illogical*! There appears to be a common thread here, and it's certainly a stitch worth picking! For within the sap or *lifeblood* of the acacia, we find an *otherworldly* chemical compound that is also found within the human body. N, N-dimethyltryptamine, or DMT, is a scientific anomaly! It permeates the natural world and is found in abundance throughout the plant and animal kingdom – but nobody quite knows why! Considered one of the world's most highly illicit psychedelics, DMT has since been dubbed *The Spirit*

Molecule after Dr. Rick Strassman's now infamous human trials which took place at the end of the last century. Strassman had theorized (and science has since confirmed) that DMT was increased in the human brain during death and near-death experiences. Classic DMT volunteer experience quotes include the following statements:

"It was familiar to me. It was like I was in the waiting room for the rebirth of souls. I was the light!"

"I didn't know whether it was my birth I was re-experiencing, my death which was yet to come, because I know that time crumbles; the linearity of time is totally meaningless in these states. You're at the Godhead, the point where all time folds in on itself!"

"There was no concept of time, it was so disorienting. I was so terrified. I have never in my life been so terrified to be blasted out of my body; to leave my body behind, to be going at warp speed backward through my own DNA, out the other end, and into the universe!"

Ethnobotanist extraordinaire, Dennis McKenna, has described DMT as a reality switch or modulator. The fact that the bandwidth of the electromagnetic spectrum which accounts for visible light is a minuscule 0.0035% of all available light certainly suggests that we might not be getting the entire proverbial picture! We're basically in the dark. What are we missing? On the face of it, it would certainly appear that somebody, somewhere had worked this out for us and inserted its profundity into myth and mortar for the benefit of future generations of humanity!

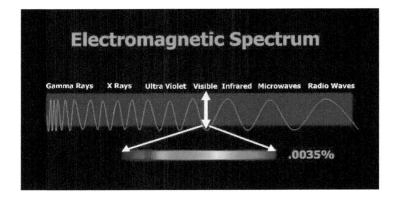

And so, we return to the Myth of Osiris.

Ancient Egyptian mythology refers to what is described as the *Djed Pillar* or *backbone of Osiris*, another archaic albeit allegorical nod towards the significance of the spinal column and the DMT therein. But further to this, the myth is extremely explicit in pointing a rather precise finger towards both the acacia and the constellation of Orion. To potentially extract DMT from within its natural habitat, it must first be drenched in a liquid before alchemically raising it from therein. This process appears to be playing out via the notion of Osiris being tossed into The Nile before being rescued/raised by his wife and lover Isis, before becoming synonymous with the constellation of Orion. If we decide to read between the lines then, there lies a rather distinct commonality between something which lies within the lifeblood or molecular structure of the acacia, and the constellation identified as Osiris in the sky. The significance of this is the two-dimensional structure of DMT being extracted from within the microcosm and broadcast across the cosmos; As Above So Below!

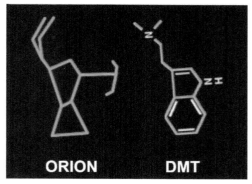

Published in 2017, *The Spirit in the Sky 'Ancient Cosmological Gods & Where In The World We Find Them'*, I hypothesized Osiris as an ancient allegory for the pineal gland. The hypothesis was further elaborated upon in the book's follow-up two years later, *DMT: Deities, Myth & Tryptamines*, whereby I proposed that Os-iris was better described as a photoreceptor within both the retina *and* the pineal gland. The chief photoreceptors are conical in appearance, like Osiris, and are green in colour; holding much in common with the cone-shaped headdress of the deity in question! We discovered that the functionality of the eyes and pineal glands rods and cones were wholly responsible for regulating or manifesting our everyday consensus reality!

Furthermore, the accompanying hieroglyph which decidedly describes Osiris rather matter-of-factly translates as follows; *Osiris, Seat of Perception!*

DMT, we find, is also present in the body's cerebrospinal fluid (Djed), lungs, eyes, and pineal gland! Furthermore, it was through the revelations of researcher Jimo Borjinin who used a technique called *in situ hybridization* which scanned the entire brain in search of the two essential enzymes which are critical for the endogenous production of DMT. These enzymes, known as INMT and AADC, were found not only in the pineal gland but also in large quantities including the neocortex and hippocampus which are responsible for modulating higher-order brain functions including learning and memory recall at levels similar to other monoamine neurotransmitters, such as serotonin and melatonin! The resulting experimentally induced cardiac arrest test subjects in rats highlighted the distinct increase in DMT concentration within the neocortex, which suggests that DMT may be considered a catalyst or key to regulating perceived levels of reality itself! So, it would appear that by way of Osiris being dismembered by his brother Seth, we are responsible for re-membering Osiris by way of constructing reality via the conical photoreceptors of the retina and pineal!

Further to the Myth of Osiris however, we encounter a daily battle for the kingdom of Egypt between Horus and Set (Seth), Horus' sworn enemy responsible for the untimely death of his father, Osiris. The tale depicts a fight (twice daily), between these forces of good and evil (light and dark) whereby Set destroys Horus at sunset and reigns over the Nile Valley by night. Horus however, avenges this loss to his nemesis at sunrise and banishes Set to the underworld until the setting sun once again. Looking at this through a rather more scientific lens altogether we learn the significance of what's being transcribed here. Serotonin may be likened to Horus, as the neurotransmitter is systematically secreted during daylight hours only. Set then, God of Darkness and Chaos is a natural contender for the neurotransmitter's chemical counterpart, melatonin, which is typically distributed to essential parts of the body by way of the pineal gland during the night or once the sun has Set. Old Kingdom texts refer to Osiris' celestial namesake Orion describing the *Mysteries of Abydos* whereby Osiris crosses The Nile via the cosmic barge known as the Neshmet. This particular star in the constellation of Leporis (the Hare) is known to astronomers today as Mu Leporis. Here then, if we decide to join the proverbial dots in the constellation of Orion/Osiris with the brightest star in the constellation of the Hare, Alpha Leporis (directly below) along with Mu Leporis/Neshmet (the cosmic barge), we create a heavenly blueprint of DMT, the *Spirit in the Sky*! This would appear to satisfy the mythology of a shared cosmology between Osiris and Wenet the hare-headed deity which manifests as a union of the two which was known to the Ancient Egyptians as Un-Nefer! Continuing our journey within the constellation of Lepus/Wenet to satisfy the mythology, there is another star that is directly associated with Osiris and the Mysteries of Abydos. Beta Leporis, we find, has an archaic namesake also; Nihal! Naturally highlighting this particularly revered star which appears to phonetically link to Osiris' journey across The Nile/Nihal, we create an altogether new molecule manifesting around the mythology – serotonin! And by way of cosmic confirmation, the star name Nihal has several ancient connotations, all of which are centered around the notion of *joyfulness*! Here then, the particular star that makes all this possible is synonymous with the functionality of the neurotransmitter it is clearly depicting! And not unlike DMT, serotonin is also produced by the pineal gland and is thus responsible for several roles within the human brain; namely creating the feeling of general well-being or joyfulness! This union, however, more broadly speaking would also complete the mythology by unifying both deities (Osiris/Wenet) as the father of the gods SAHU – *the hidden one* or *incorruptible soul*! As above so

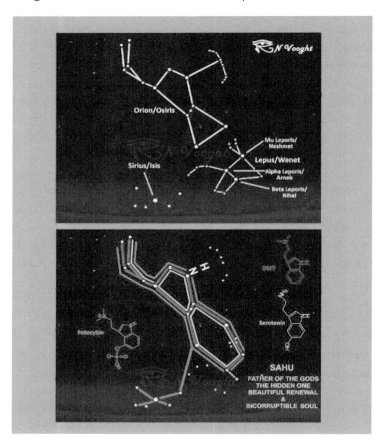

below!! it would certainly appear that through ancient allegory, myth, and metaphor, due to the biomechanical functionality of the brain and its interaction with photons of light via parts of the brain such as the eyes and visual cortex that the ever-present anomaly DMT, may, in fact, prove key or catalyst to how to perceive the world around us! Indeed, ethnobotanist Dennis McKenna has likened the DMT experience to a reality switch that is essentially responsible for modulating the sensory input from the outside world around us – the wizard behind the curtain, as it were. We must remember that DMT is a natural phenomenon that permeates the plant and animal kingdom, it's simply everywhere! And Strassman's research volunteers may have been privy to a whole new world of universal understanding. Well, we're certainly not in Kansas anymore! Moreover, there's an almost obvious and ever-apparent common thread that cross-pollinates cultures and customs the globe over regarding the mythological Tree of Life; the fingerprints of which appear to point towards the highly revered acacia variety, and the so-called gods hidden within! Further to the tale of Osiris, lies the otherwise unfathomable anomaly that is the Osirion in Abydos, Egypt; a temple construction which has been loosely dated to around 12,000 years BP, and the natural phenomenon that is DMT, all seemingly suggest a point of origin which connects them with the oldest known structure as yet uncovered in the guarded world of archaeology – Gobekli Tepe!

THE UMBILICAL OF OSIRIS

Until relatively recently, it was understood that civilized high society was established no more than five thousand years or so ago; whereby the chronology of the documented human story evolved from prehistoric hunter-gatherers to the birth of dynastic Ancient Egypt sometime around 3100 BCE. Best-selling authors such as Graham Hancock and John Anthony West et al had often argued a case for a far earlier epoch of human ingenuity lost to the modern memory of the accepted narrative. Said authors, had been subjected to a bombardment of ridicule because of the lack of so-called evidence therein; despite the often-rejected claims by the Ancient Egyptians themselves who remained convinced of an ancestral lineage that stretched beyond the bounds of what the 'experts' deemed possible. Described as Zep Tepi, meaning the First Time, Ancient Egyptian mythology describes a kind of Golden Era of accumulated understanding which had been catalogued approximately thirty-six thousand years before that which Egyptologists were currently willing to acknowledge. On the face of it, Egyptological ideals remained adamant that they know more about the pre-pharaonic predecessors than the Ancient Egyptians themselves, once again citing the lack of evidence of anything which may have come before. Entre, Gobekli Tepe.

Gobekli Tepe, classically translated as *pot-bellied hill*, is a Neolithic archaeological site near the city of Sanliurfa in South Eastern Anatolia, Turkey. It does, however, also go by a far more archaic Ancient Armenian agname; Portasar which translates as the *Umbilical of Osiris*. And as thus our myth continues.

Gobekli Tepe, we find, is a twelve-thousand-year-old ancient anomaly that appears to defy everything we previously thought possible. This vast complex of ancient architecture was constructed sometime around the end of the last Mini Ice Age known as the Younger Dryas Period and rather bizarrely, it seems to have been intentionally buried to preserve its rather extraordinary significance. It has come to light, through the extensive and now largely accepted research of Dr. Martin Sweatman, that the otherwise confusing arrangement of animal carvings that adorn the most famous T-shaped pillars enclosed within the complex, might represent a turning point (or backward step) in civilized society 12,000 years ago by way of a previously undocumented cataclysm, which current research postulates via some kind of untimely celestial impact. Even more astonishing, however, we find that the depictions in question were carved in three-dimensional high-relief iconography which wasn't deemed possible until another 6000 years or so. Furthermore, the much-debated anthropomorphic pillars which are typically stylized with human arms which appear to embrace the monoliths share a great deal in common with the famous Easter Island carvings of the Moai.

Almost everyone is readily familiar with the iconic Moai, 900 or so of which are scattered about the island, yet most are blissfully unaware that these colossal carvings do have entire torsos buried beneath thousands of years of naturally deposited sediment. Classically speaking, the traditionalists claim that the islanders crafted these stone sculptures in three distinct

From Easter Island to Gobekli Tepe

Above Left to Right: Easter Island Moai, Tiwanaku & Gobekli Tepe

Above Left: Moai & Gobekli Tepe pillar

Above Centre: Full Moai torso unearthed

Above Right: Gobekli Tepe pillar pelt

Left: Seshat, Ancient Egyptian Goddess of Writing wearing Gobekli Tepe-like pelt

RN Vooght

phases of occupation, the earliest being dated to around 700-850 AD. The timeline of which appears to be somewhat problematic due to the nature of the earliest and only known scripture accredited to its inhabitants. Affectionately described as the Rongorongo script; a type of proto-writing 'adopted' by its indigenous community, shares an uncanny number of commonalities with an as-yet-undeciphered writing system employed by a relatively unknown civilization from the Indus Valley almost 12,500 miles away – a subject we shall return to in due course! Moreover, the Indus Valley's Harappan Script is officially documented as being in use between 3500-1900 BCE, and the so-called coincidences don't stop here either; because the antipode (geographic and global opposite) of Easter Island is none other than the Indus Valley! And rather astonishingly, we find that the Moai bodies (or more specifically, their backs) appear to depict the same celestial bombardment and archaic embrace as what we witness in Gobekli Tepe! Yet even more intriguingly, the waistline pelt or animal skin adorned by the T-pillared persona can be found draped across the torso of the Ancient Egyptian deity, Seshat; a Goddess of Writing, no less! So, the question begging to be asked here is; is there another clear and present connection between Gobekli Tepe and the Ancient Egyptians? You bet there is! In the first book of the series, we discovered how the Great Pyramid can be considered a hemispheric model of the earth to a ratio of 43,200/1, and that there are 43,200 seconds of daylight during the equinoxes. We also understand that there are 86,400 seconds in a day and that the accepted diameter of the sun is 864,000 miles across. What also became apparent is that the Great Pyramid itself appears to be a construction dedicated to the notion of *light*, whereby the significance of its latitudinal location (29.9792458 N) is symbolic of the speed of light (299,792,458 meters per second). This particular discovery is much debated, but is further reinforced by the fact that a circle drawn in meters within the base structure of the pyramid subtracted from the circumference of a circle drawn around the perimeter of its base, also dictates the speed of light! Further to this, however, recent mathematical calculations also appear to correlate the longitudinal coordinates of the Great Pyramid alongside the mean diameter of the sun! By simply dividing the monument's longitude reference of 31.134667 E by 360 (31.134667 / 360 = 0.0864) we arrive at a figure which is definitively associated with light also! And as we discovered earlier in the series, the Great Pyramid is actually guilty of displaying eight sides instead of the four which most are readily familiar with. The profundity of which was revealed via the striking likeness to the cross-section of a photon of light! The deviating slope incline which creates the eight-sided edifice when viewed from above has been calculated to be precisely .432 degrees! The Ancient Egyptian god, Amun, is a solar deity who is synonymous with the Great Pyramid; Amun is a phonetic variation of Amen which the bible will tell us is Jesus – the light of the world and the Son/Sun of God! In the second book of the series, we uncovered a plethora of correlations that regarded Jesus and Os-iris as the same archaic axiom for light and the photoreceptors of the eyes and pineal gland (the light receptor of the human body). Osiris, we find, has a temple dedicated to his name in Abydos. The Osirion is considered an Ancient Egyptian anomaly, due in part to the much-debated timeline of the construction. Lying semi-submerged below the bedrock, the Osirion is typically dated to

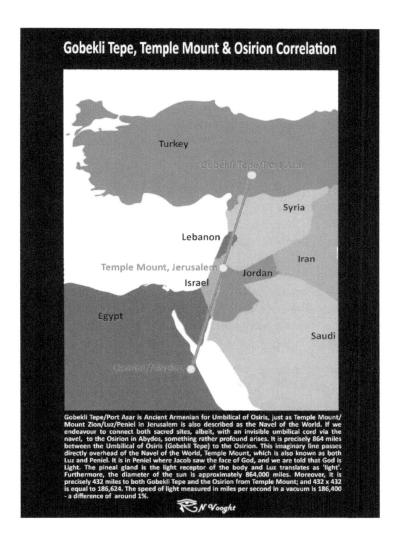

Gobekli Tepe, Temple Mount & Osirion Correlation

Gobekli Tepe/Port Asar is Ancient Armenian for Umbilical of Osiris, just as Temple Mount/ Mount Zion/Luz/Peniel in Jerusalem is also described as the Navel of the World. If we endeavour to connect both sacred sites, albeit, with an invisible umbilical cord via the navel, to the Osirion in Abydos, something rather profound arises. It is precisely 864 miles between the Umbilical of Osiris (Gobekli Tepe) to the Osirion. This imaginary line passes directly overhead of the Navel of the World, Temple Mount, which is also known as both Luz and Peniel. It is in Peniel where Jacob saw the face of God, and we are told that God is Light. The pineal gland is the light receptor of the body and Luz translates as 'light'. Furthermore, the diameter of the sun is approximately 864,000 miles. Moreover, it is precisely 432 miles to both Gobekli Tepe and the Osirion from Temple Mount; and 432 x 432 is equal to 186,624. The speed of light measured in miles per second in a vacuum is 186,400 - a difference of around 1%.

N Vooght

have been constructed by Seti i sometime around 1250 BC, although many believe it to be far older. It is often touted as possibly being some 12,000 years old, the same date as Gobelki Tepe which we know to also be called Portasar – the Umbilical of Osiris! Now, if we decide to draw an imaginary line, cord, or indeed umbilical between the two locations something curiously intriguing is revealed. The distance between these Osiris-identifiable anomalies is precisely 864 miles – its significance once again relative to the dimensions of the sun! And almost inexplicably, this imaginary umbilical not only crosses directly over the biblical city of Jerusalem but a little less than a mile shy of 432 miles is the fabled Temple Mount and the Dome of the Rock! The Dome of the Rock is built on top of the Foundation Stone, which is sacred to both Jews and Muslims. Islamic belief dictates it as the site at which the prophet Muhammad's ascension to heaven took place. According to Jewish tradition, the stone is considered the "navel of the Earth"—the place where creation began; ironically tying our umbilical to the metaphorical naval itself! The question then arises, however; could this Temple Mount and place of creation also be

the root of the same sacred mound for which Osiris is typically associated? Described as the *Tree of Life* we understand that the oldest sandstone Stella depicting the name of Osiris is also inscribed with an acacia tree atop the hill of creation. The significance of the acacia we know to be mythologically associated as the lifeblood of Osiris and the otherworldly entheogen contained within. And as if they reinforce the notion of an entheogenic ideology hidden within, the Ancient Arabian and pre-Islamic Goddess of Strength, Healing, and Protection; Al-Uzza was deified, like Osiris, as manifesting from within the confines of the acacia. Furthermore, this central figurehead throughout the culture who is often typified as establishing the ancient city of Petra was also considered the complete embodiment of the belt stars of Orion – our two-dimensional macroscopic mind-altering molecule DMT! Returning to the Osirian however, what are the chances then, that the only inscription found here depicts the sacred and wholly geometric *Flower of Life*? The Osirion itself defies explanation. Most of its construction materials were sourced and quarried in Aswan almost 200 miles away, some of which weigh in excess of 100 tonnes! Inscribed some eight feet or so above the base of one of these impressive supporting pillars is the iconic *Flower of Life*. An image that has become a somewhat global phenomenon due to its presence throughout ancient architecture from almost every sophisticated society known to the historical narrative. But why? What could this interconnected understanding be symbolic of? The nature of reality, maybe? DMT is rapidly being considered as a neurotransmitter; an essential chemical, albeit psychoactive, compound described as a reality switch. A switch whereby consensus reality is modulated via the external information which enters the visual cortex via the interaction of photons of light that pass through the retina. In the second book of the series, we discovered a wealth of commonalities between the headdress and torso of Osiris and the chief photoreceptors within the human eye and pineal gland, and their otherwise inexplicable connection to DMT found therein. Rather remarkably, classically reported closed and open-eyed visuals during the DMT experience share extraordinary parallels with the geometric structure of the Flower of Life – and possibly reality itself! Could this hypervivid and entity-rich alternate reality,

DMT, Osiris & The Flower of Life

The Osirian in Abydos, Egypt, depicting the Flower of Life.

The Flower of Life.

Rendition of classic geometric visuals during DMT experience.

Here Osiris is depicted as the lifeblood of the acacia. The acacia variety is known for its extracable DMT potential therein.

actually be host to the ever-present reports of highly intelligent 'beings' often referred to in ancient accounts of immaterial 'others' acting as a guiding hand throughout the evolution of the species? Ancient linguist and fellow writer and researcher Laird Scranton has proposed that the high-relief carvings witnessed at Gobekli Tepe describe a symbolic train of thought which would not look out of place were it scribbled upon the whiteboards of modern-day physicists. Scranton has revealed that the relatively unknown cosmology of an ancient nomadic culture known as the Dogon and the oldest writings of the Buddhist religion, do share several otherworldly commonalities and characteristics which hold true to scientific understandings, that have otherwise inadvertently been cast aside and ignored by the mainstream mentality. Both classically unconnected cultures do however appear to also share a point of origin which at the outset seemingly defies explanation. Until now. It is understood that the most sacred and significant teachings of Buddhist cosmology allow their collective knowledge to have been bestowed upon them by an otherwise non-human source. The ancient, yet modern-day tribespeople of the Dogon however, share an unparalleled cosmology with their Buddhist counterparts in almost every aspect bar the source. The Dogon appears to go one step further by way of suggesting that their cosmology was imparted to them via a non-material source! Both trains of thought inadvertently share a logical understanding regarding the nature of the cosmos which has since been underpinned by science itself. But what can be said of the origins of said teachings? Laird Scranton expertly elaborates upon this by revealing that both cosmologies adhere to the notion that the universe in which we exist was born into being alongside an immaterial twin universe; whereby those occupying the material realm of consensus reality have an imperfect understanding of the nature of reality but an ability to act upon their thoughts and desires, but the immaterial 'other' has a complete and perfect understanding but an inability to act. And like an hourglass, when the sands of time are perfectly balanced albeit aligned, both of these co-dependant realities reach a threshold where they are deemed somewhat equal, and limited interaction with one another may take place. All of which has been meticulously inscribed upon the pillars of the world's oldest temple – Gobekli Tepe!

Scranton goes on to eloquently discuss how the notion of an embrace alongside the H-shaped symbology at the site suggests the coming together of material and immaterial realities which are co-dependent upon each other. Throughout our deep dive into antiquity, we have discovered that all of the world's most popular belief systems adhere to the notion that God is light. The fact that light is considered massless deems it immaterial by nature. The act of observing photons, we are told, manifests material reality into existence. At present, scientists are at a loss to answer why the process of observing a photon of light makes the photon in question act as both a wave and a particle. It's both material and immaterial. But because we need to interact with light in order to manifest the world around us, it's extremely intriguing to find that the light visible to the human eye accounts for a minuscule 0.0035% of the electromagnetic spectrum. So, what else are we missing? Could there be an ultra-terrestrial world of understanding hidden in plain sight? DMT psychonauts seem to agree with the existence of an unparalleled metaphysical, albeit immaterial reality inhabited by highly evolved entities beyond the threshold of our own material existence. And hearsay aside, the Ancients referred to these sometimes immaterial 'others' as the *Shining Ones*, an otherwise mythological and magical manifestation of multidimensional masters of material reality who have helped humankind during an unknowable antiquity from Ancient Egypt to the South American Altiplano.

THE SHINING FOLLOWERS OF HORUS

In keeping with Ancient Egyptian mythology, we learn that Osiris' legacy and the kingdom of the ancient Nile were left to his son, Horus. Horus, we find, is a falcon-headed deity – falcons are revered for their extraordinary vision. It is said that the deity's eyes represented both the sun and the moon; the latter of which was lost during a battle with his late father's nemesis and evil uncle, Set. We discussed the ever-present commonalities between the iconic Eye of Horus talisman, the Ancient Egyptian 'Vault of Heaven' and the human brain stem in *The Spirit in the Sky*; and it remains clear that the allegorical nature of our ancient ancestors are trying to point us in the direction of profundity instead of the absurdity being peddled by its current keepers. As we have seen, there is a curious connection between Gobekli Tepe and the Osirion which could well prove that the Osirion itself is at least 12,000 years old. What if the same could be said of the pyramids of the Giza Plateau? The Great Pyramid quite rightfully overshadows the smaller but no less impressive constructions in its wake, but for the sake of our current investigation, we shall briefly focus upon the Pyramid of Menkaure. Much like the two larger pyramids of the plateau, the Pyramid of Menkaure is also lacking in major inscriptions. It is understood and agreed upon, that the pyramid is also dedicated to the Falcon god, Horus. It is of note that a pre-dynastic cult known as the *Aku Shemsu Hor* translates as the *Shining Followers of Horus*. With this in mind, the pyramid does, however, display a rather perplexing anomaly. The lowest and first handful of major courses of construction is remarkably similar (if not precisely the same) to what we witness in the Andes almost 7,500 miles away! The smooth and interlocking construction technique along with the distinct and somewhat distracting nubs which appear on them are ever-present throughout Sacsayhuaman. The classic and accepted timeline of the historical narrative remains blinkered regarding the possibility that these ancient civilizations were ever connected. However, should we dare to consider that the oldest 'accepted' temple construction on the face of the planet (Gobekli Tepe) is dedicated to the Ancient Egyptian deity, Osiris, and we endeavour to connect the two via an invisible umbilical once again, we find that distance between the two sites are approximated as the earth's mean diameter of 7,920 miles! And it's here where it starts to really get interesting. Sacsayhuaman is described as a Peruvian outpost whose original functionality is largely unknown. Accredited to the Inca Empire which was toppled and devastated by the arrival of the Spanish Conquistadores in the 16th century, the earliest occupation of the site is usually dated to around 900 CE. This vast and expansive complex however is constructed of interlocking and mortarless polygonal masonry blocks, some of which weigh more than 200 tonnes! A direct translation of the Quechua word, Sacsayhuaman, offers us an intriguing insight into its original builders and a direct link back to the Menkhure pyramid of the Giza Plateau. Sacsayhuaman means 'Place of the Satisfied Falcon', which would certainly appear to suggest its connection back to the so-called son of Osiris, Horus! Furthermore, legend has it that the celebrated deity of the region, Viracocha, was considered a solar God whose appearance was white-skinned and bearded, who arrived after a major cataclysm with his seven 'Shining Ones' to aid humanity with the skills necessary to rise from the aforementioned catastrophe! And once again, the

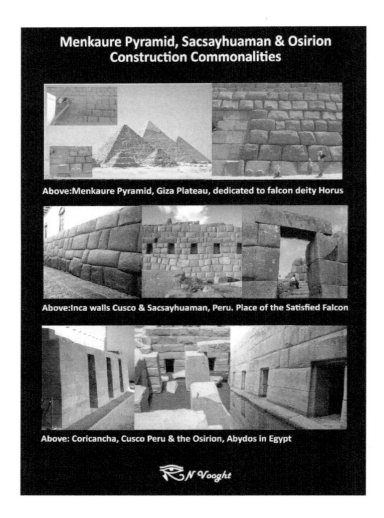

Menkaure Pyramid, Sacsayhuaman & Osirion Construction Commonalities

Above: Menkaure Pyramid, Giza Plateau, dedicated to falcon deity Horus

Above: Inca walls Cusco & Sacsayhuaman, Peru. Place of the Satisfied Falcon

Above: Coricancha, Cusco Peru & the Osirion, Abydos in Egypt

N Vooght

archaic foundations of Tiwanaku in neighbouring Bolivia we find are still accredited to the Inca Empire, who clearly restored them by adding to it with a far-lesser refined construction technique to an already existing superior template. The so-called Sun Gate at Tiwanaku for example, would not look of place at the Osirion almost half the world away! Their similarities certainly don't stop there as we also find T-shaped false doors described as gates or portals into the Spirit World, which are cut into rockfaces and are eerily reminiscent of the deified T-pillars of Gobekli Tepe. The free-standing pillars of ancient Anatolia seem to depict an otherwise mystifying H-shaped motif emblazoned across their navel area which has been quite rightly likened to the mysteriously masterful masonry of the interlinking H-blocks of Puma Punku, in Tiwanaku. The name Tiwanaku is an Aymara word meaning 'my people', but it also appears to carry an Ancient Egyptian syllable along with it – *aku* meaning 'shining'. Therefore, it may be considered that Tiwanaku could translate as 'My Shining People'! Here then, we have several direct correlations between both Ancient Egypt and the Andes. It should also be noted that the builder of the Great Pyramid (whomever Khufu was or indeed whenever Khufu was) was called Aaku Khufu which again is understood to be linked to the notion of light! And for the sake of our particular line of inquiry, and for reasons unbeknown to archaeologists and despite their silence upon the matter, it is a known if not otherwise perplexing fact that significant traces of tobacco and cocaine have been found within mummified bodies of deceased Ancient Egyptian hierarchy. An oddity in the extreme when we consider such substances to be native to the Americas! We shall return our investigation to the notion of the dead, or indeed, the resurrected in due course, but for all intents and purposes, we shall continue our search for Osiris in Central and South America. Viracocha, we find has several names and was known to the Mayan and Aztec civilizations as Kukulkan or Quetzalcoatl. A literal translation is 'Feathered Serpent'; which brings into question (or correlation) another trans-Atlantic phenomenon of the Ancient Egyptian headdress or uraeus, which classically depicts both a falcon and snake above the brow which rests anatomically in line with the mystical third eye or pineal gland. And rather extraordinarily, this ancient deity's calling card is still used today throughout the western world, and more specifically, throughout the medical fraternity. Known today as the *caduceus* (Ancient Geek for a *wand*) its iconography is that of a staff entwined between two rising serpents which meet the outstretched wings atop; its wholly metaphorical revelation subtly reminding us of the DMT-rich cerebrospinal fluid which rises from the base of the spine in a serpentine motion thus bathing the left and right hemispheres of the brain (cerebrum/cherubim/wings); which we discussed in the second book of the series. In the first book of the series, we discovered the profound and purely allegorical nature of the Ancient Egyptian cosmology regarding the legacy of their chosen *tree of life*. Here then, we rather unequivocally answered the many reasons why the myth of Osiris was established with such authority alongside the entheogenic properties of the acacia; so, with Ancient Egypt appearing to hold so much common-ground with the deities and mythologies of the ancient Andes and beyond, it was only natural to ask if the same could be said regarding the roots of the Incan, Mayan, and Aztec cosmology also. And what we find is (3rd) eye-opening to state the very least!

OTHERWORLDS

The Mayan *Tree of Life* holds much in common with Ancient Egyptian mythology, whereby the tree of choice, the Ceiba, was said to be responsible for holding the entire universe within it. Moreover, the Ceiba (aka the Ya'axche) was wholly symbolic of the axis mundi which connected the *underworld* and the cosmos with the terrestrial plane we fondly call reality. The underworld, or Xibalba, roughly translates as *the place of fear*, insomuch that it was the Gods of Death who were said to reside within it. Here then, it would appear to mirror the mythological lore of the Nile Valley; as we also understand that it was the God of Resurrection, Osiris, who dwelt within the confines of the acacia tree and ruled over the souls of the deceased in the realms of the underworld known as the Fields of Aaru. Aaru, we find, is also described by the Ancient Greeks as the Field of Reeds – to which this investigation will slowly gravitate towards answering why! For now, however, it is vital to understand that the chosen Mayan *Tree of Life*, not unlike the Ancient Egyptian *acacia*, is extremely rich in the 'otherworldly' chemical compound N, N dimethyltryptamine – our Spirit Molecule, DMT! Also highly revered for its consciousness-altering analogues hidden within, is the sacred Vine of Souls known locally as Ayahuasca. This ancient Amazonian shamanic tool holds much in common with pre-Renaissance period artwork which describes the same kind of spiritual ascension which sees mortal souls and saints alike, enter a heavenly plane amongst the realm of the Gods! The example expressed here from the 12th century depicts the Ladder of Di(vine) Ascent from the St Catherine's Monastery from the Sinai Peninsula, Egypt, no less; whereby Jesus/Osiris is pictured waiting atop! Another Pre-Columbian and Mayan creator deity who appears to reflect the myth of Osiris is Itzamna; a creator God,

Renaissance Period Artwork & Ayahuasca

Above: Ladder of Di-vine Ascent & Auahuasca Vine of the Amazon Basin.
Below: Jacob's Ladder by Willam Blake & Amazonian twin serpent artwork allegorical of DNA double helix.

Pre Columbian artwork depicting Anadenanthra Colubrina seeds containing Bufotenine, 5-MEO DMT & NN-DMT

Above: Note top left box which clearly appears to depict purging which is wholly common with ayahuasca ingestion.

Above: Machine Elves?

ruler of Heaven and day and night. In the second book of this series, we discussed the potentiality of Osiris being metaphoric of DMT and the pineal gland, which is responsible for secreting essential hormones into the body's circularity system. We also enquired as to the likelihood of Horus and Set being allegorical of said hormones serotonin and melatonin, which are secreted during daylight hours and darkness respectively. It's curious then to discover that the etymology of Itzamna shares the same characteristics as the myth of Osiris. In The Spirit in the Sky, we uncovered the profound nature of a mythological God who is likened to the lifeblood or sap of the acacia; notwithstanding the entire magical lore of resurrection and a plane of existence beyond the scope of our everyday perception. Rather intriguingly, we find, that the prefix *'Itza'* translates as both *'magic'* and *'sap'*! Connotations surely abound! Let us not forget that the Mayan 'otherworld' was also described as being hidden within the constellation of Orion – Orion itself being described as a gateway to the Gods! DMT, anyone?

If this particular train of thought was in any doubt, however, one of the most celebrated and iconic depictions of the Mayan Tree of Life depicts the act of purging or vomiting in the upper realm; the act of purging being wholly indicative of ingesting the trees sacred secretion more commonly termed as Ayahuasca. Here then, our ancient ancestry was trying to reflect the fact that this particular methodology is more than mere coincidence. The ever-present anthropomorphic iconography can surely only be equated to the interdimensional deities this otherworldly intoxicant reveals to the initiate therein.

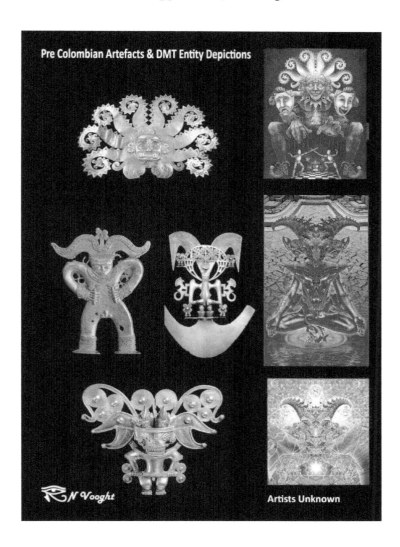

Pre Colombian Artefacts & DMT Entity Depictions

N Vooght

Artists Unknown

Moreover, the DMT deity archetypes, albeit machine elves and jesters, appear to be extremely commonplace regarding pre-Colombian artifacts also. The examples pictured depict the much-famed trickster profiles witnessed upon many breakthrough doses of DMT! Not a great deal is known about these otherworldly artifacts which continue to defy rational explanation. However, what we can be certain of is the fact that the region was, and largely still is, practicing a tried and tested methodology regarding their own sacred plant-based secretion. Anadenanthrea Colubrina is a psychoactive variety whose seeds are known to contain Bufotenine, 5-MEO-DMT, and NN-DMT. And because of the uncanny connotations which go hand in hand with these psychoactive super-substances, the otherwise mythical notion somewhat loosely termed as El Dorado, may well be better described as the DMT realm itself. The artifacts thems(elves) serving as a timeless reminder of what waits for us beyond the material bonds of everyday waking reality within the framework of the DMT experience! Thus, it becomes extremely evident that the creators of the artefact were clearly depicting the archetypal jester-like machine elves which have become much-famed via first-hand breakthrough reports in recent years. Researcher and ethnobotanist Dennis McKenna adds further weight to this proposal via the archaeological discovery which suggests that DMT use was central to the Tiwanaku culture in the north of Bolivia and pre-Incan cultures of Peru. The Ponce monolith figure found in the Tiwanaku complex holds two ritual objects, a snuffing tablet and a pouch with tubes used for ingesting the powdered Villca seeds (Anadenanthera Colubrina). The archaeological findings in the nearby areas confirm that the equipment for the inhalation of psychoactive powders usually consists of a small tray, a snuffing tube, a spoon, and leather pouches as containers for the powders. The patterns of Villca seeds found on the statue also suggest that its use was central to the Tiwanaku culture.

All of a sudden, the original hypothesis regarding the myth of Osiris being an archaic axiom for As Above So Below as a formula to unite a microcosmic and molecular understanding reflected upon the cosmos as a two-dimensional template of DMT within the structure of Orion/Osiris, doesn't seem to appear too outlandish.

On the contrary. The Ancient Mayan, Aztec, and Inca civilizations also highlight their own 'otherworldly' constellation which more than mirrors the myth of Osiris. The Chakana, or Andean Cross, is

Southern Crux
&
Inca Chakana Symbology

Central to Ancient Inca cosmology the Chakana is symbolic of the Southern Cross constellation.

The word Chakana is based on the word "chakay," which means "to cross" or "to bridge".

The symbol is often constructed in such a way that only half of it protrudes from architechtural structures; the cross is thus completed by its shadow created by the sun. The shadow representing the non-material world.

The Chakana is also considered symboloic of the Tree of Life; a cosmology which is further reinforced by way of Mimosa - a variety of acacia with significant potentials of the otherworldy chemical compound DMT.

Southern Crux

Mimosa

N Vooght

a stepped cross which is said to be symbolic of the Tree of Life and the three levels of existence known as the Hana Pacha (the Upper World inhabited by the Gods), the Kay Pacha (the/our world of everyday existence), and the Ukha (an Underworld inhabited by the Spirits of deceased ancestors and deities with direct access to the Kay Pacha). The hole in the center of the Chakana is said to act as a mode of transit or portal by which the shaman may access the other immaterial planes of existence. The etymology of the Chakana is rather revealing too, as the native Quechua language describes the prefix 'Chaka' as a 'bridge' or a means to 'cross over'!

One of the main focal points regarding this particular deep dive into antiquity is to show the ever-present fingerprint of a wholly-connected global understanding regarding humanity's all too obvious hidden history. Rather remarkably, the significance of the Chakana symbology isn't strictly limited to the South American Andes. On the contrary, for recent discoveries made within the Indus Valley, Northwest India, there appears to be a shared methodology regarding these two otherwise 'unconnected' cultures. Classically described as the Harappan civilization which flourished between 3300BC and 1900BC, the Harappan share an absurdly similar system of script with those of Easter Island, over two thousand miles off the coast of South American, Peru! The traditional timeline of Easter Island and its inhabitants is rather ridiculously recalled by archaeologists to be sometime around 700AD. Notwithstanding the fact that world-famous Moai statues share a plethora of uncanny carvings found at Gobekli Tepe/Port Asar which are typically dated to around 12,000 years ago! The Moai themselves were buried almost up to their necks before archaeologists discovered that they did have entire torsos freakishly familiar with the T-shaped pillars of the Gobekli Tepe

Indus Valley & Easter Island Commonalities

Indus Valley & Rongorongo script, Easter Island

Easter Island Moai, Gobekli Tepe & Tiwanaku

Indus Valley seals & global Chakana carvings

enclosures in modern-day Turkey. So, it's hardly surprising then, that the Rongorongo script and that of the Harappan are almost identical also! Even more astonishing, we find, that burial sites across the Indus Valley are unearthing intricately inscribed seals used to guide the recently deceased between realms with what can only be described as the Ancient South American talisman, the Chakana! The significance of this is continually being ignored by the mainstream mindset. The fact the Harappan were using this ancient iconography in wholly the same context as their South American counterparts is absolutely astonishing!

Furthermore, the constellation which is wholly symbolic of the Chakana is known today as the Southern Crux/Cross; moreover, the brightest star in this particular grouping is recognized as Mimosa which is a variety of acacia with highly extractable potentials of DMT – the essential ingredient to the shamanic intoxicant Ayahuasca! And it's here where the all too obvious profundity of fellow researcher and writer Jeremy Narby's conclusions appear to somewhat bolster my own brave blueprint of an ancient understanding of the nature of reality and the microscopic world of mind-manifesting molecules traversed by the indigenous shaman of the Amazonian Basin! Narby's ground-breaking title *The Cosmic Serpent* was originally published in 1995 after the Canadian anthropologist originally undertook an investigation into the native people's protection and sustainability of their rainforest habitat. But the subsequent line of inquiry was soon redirected instead towards the revelations of the indigenous shamanic know-how regarding an unprecedented insight into the botanical molecular biology of the Amazon! The Ashaninka shaman appeared to be privy to a world beyond our own perception and remained steadfast that their phenomenal knowledge of the botanical varieties around which they were surrounded, was in fact, imparted to them by the plant spirits themselves while under the influence of the hallucinogenic properties extracted from their chosen *tree of life*! Further to this, however, Narby realized the profundity of the now all-too-obvious significance regarding the ever-present twin serpent symbolism as a metaphor for a modern understanding of biochemistry we know as DNA! The shaman described their inexplicable plant-based communications as a 'language-twisting-twisting' as if it were the DNA itself imparting its undeniable understanding of its own molecular make-up. And it appeared to be an archaic yet global phenomenon. Countless examples of this are found around the world whereby iconography of entwined serpents, braided ropes, and spiral ladders are depicted as a stairway between the realms of the material and immaterial alike. Take the Ancient Egyptian iconography of the Cosmic Serpent known as the 'provider of attributes' for example; the glyphs that accompany this twin-headed (entwined) serpent directly translate as 'spirit', 'double', 'vital force' and 'water'. Underneath the chin of said serpents is the Ancient Egyptian cross or 'Ankh' which is symbolic of the 'Key of Life', and Narby would certainly appear to be correct when stating that its connections with DNA are obvious and that they work on all levels revealing, 'DNA is shaped like a long, single and double serpent, or a wick of twisted flax; it is a vital force that develops from one to several; its place is water!'. And Narby's well-founded overview gives raise to the question; Why are these metaphors so consistently and so frequently used unless they mean what they say? Rather intriguingly, we find that this shamanic methodology of describing molecules by way of a mind-manifesting mixture of mythology and allegorical allure has been repeated via one of the most ancient and otherwise isolated cultures on the face of the planet.

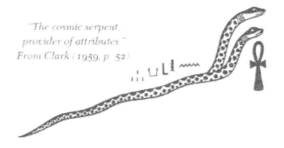

"The cosmic serpent,
provider of attributes "
From Clark (1959, p 52).

This Ancient Egyptian drawing does not represent a real animal, but a visual charade meaning "double serpent."

DREAMTIME & THE RAINBOW BRIDGE

Native Australian symbology depicted by the Dreamtime narrative of the Aboriginal peoples holds much in common with both South American shaman and our original line of investigation, the myth of Osiris. Dating back some 65,000 years or so, the Aboriginal Tree of Life mythology is centered around the sacred Yarran or white gum tree. This particular variety is also a part of the acacia family and is wholly symbolic of the constellation the Southern Cross. Legend has it that at the beginning of time when Baiame, the Sky Spirit walked the Earth, He molded the first humans out of the red earth and brought them to life (the same fabled creation story familiar to Christianity which also appears to be somewhat borrowed from the Ancient Egyptian story of creator deity Amun). Further to the story, however, the first human to know death was found by his peers at the foot of the Yarran tree with Yowie, the Spirit of Death. Yowie, it is said, lifted the dead fellow and placed him within the hollowed trunk of the tree, before a deafening burst of thunder and lightning set it ablaze and lifted it skyward until it disappeared from view and was replaced by the constellation of the Southern Cross! The parallels regarding the myth of Osiris are quite remarkable; the body of Osiris was entombed within the trunk of the acacia before he was resurrected as the constellation of Orion/DMT. And rather uncannily, the dot-like depictions which describe these Aboriginal tales known as the Dreamtime, are not unlike the microscopic world of molecular structures familiar to the worlds of both 21st-century chemists, biologists, and those of their South American counterparts exposed via Jeremy Narby! Stranger

still, the otherwise hidden credence of said Dreamtime storyline also speaks of Rainbow Serpents and the notion of humanity's lifeforce arising from water! At first glance, the Australian outback might appear somewhat baron and lacking in its fondly adopted nickname - Bush. But just like the famous Christian myths where God speaks with Moses from within the midst of the burning bush, the Aboriginal territories are littered with DMT analogues also. I really don't believe that it's a bridge too far to suggest that these and other mythologies hold a common train of thought. And speaking of bridges, the roots of the Ancient Scandinavian and Norse Tree of Life curiously crossover the same entheogenic ideologies.

The underlying foundations of Norse mythology are rooted within the metaphorical nature of the Tree of Life, and are littered with our old friend the pine cone; from which we derive the term pineal. Traditionally depicted as a common yew tree, the sacred path to Yggdrasil is commonly associated with Bi-Frost – the so-called shimmering path known as the Rainbow Bridge! Legend has it, that Bi-Frost is protected by Heimdall; a tall white, bearded God with an extraordinary sense of foreknowledge and vision. Heimdall, we find, is the keeper of Gjallarhorn – a single blast of which could be heard across *all the worlds*! Could this otherworldly horn then, be a metaphor for the all-encompassing resonance which appears to precede the so-called DMT breakthrough experience? The often-complex nature of Norse mythology surrounding the dual nature of the Gjallarhorn would certainly suggest so because it was spoken of in terms of a drinking vessel also. It said that whoever drank from the Gjallarhorn would be bestowed with an untold wealth of wisdom and insight, which on the outset appears to reflect an ayahuasca-type analogue also described by shamanic traditions throughout the Amazon Basin. Further to this, however, the Gjallarhorn shares another ever-apparent cosmology with the Norse god or 'being' *Mimir*. Mimir, *the Rememberer*, is described as a horned being and deified guardian of Yggdrasil who kept watch over the Well of Wisdom which was considered to be beneath the Tree of Life itself. We discussed the mythological profoundly regarding the now scientific nature of Pegasus in *Deities, Myth & Tryptamines*, and the horned nature of the hippocampus (hippocampus being Ancient Greek for Seahorse), and its all too obvious functionality certainly appears to be being portrayed here also! A brief recap on this methodology, sees Pegasus striking open the mythological well/fountain of knowledge upon Mount Helicon whereby he would become forever favoured by Mnemosyne – the Greek Goddess of Memory. The kicker here quite being literally, the *pes hippocampus'* structure looks exactly like the hoof of a horse!

Yggdrasil is also commonly and closely associated with Odin's horse no less! Moreover, it said that Odin sacrificed one of his eyes in order to drink and gain untold insight from the well of Mimir from the Gjallarhorn itself! Further to this, however, the same commonalities also seem to reflect the Ancient Egyptian mythology whereby the son of Osiris, Horus, loses an eye after which it becomes synonymous with profound insight more often depicted as the so-called 'all seeing eye'. It was in the first book of the series, however, that we discovered the all too apparent didactic nature of this talisman depicting human brain anatomy; more specifically, the cerebellum, corpus callosum, thalamus, pituitary, and pineal gland! During Odin's quest for knowledge at the foot of the Tree of Life, legend has it that he hanged himself from the branches of Yggdrasil before being lanced by a spear that

Norse Mythology

Above Left: Heimdall with the Gjallarhorn and caduceus
Above Center: Odin kills Mimir amongst the reeds
Above Right: Asgard, Yggdrasil and Bifrost bridge

Above Left: The Gjallarhorn
Above Right: Odin hanging upon Yggdrasil to gain foresight and wisdom
Left: Mimir and the Gjallarhorn

RN Vooght

was fashioned from the tree itself – all before being metaphorically resurrected thereafter. A story which again seemingly reflects that of Jesus who was hung upon a cross and lanced in the side before miraculously walking out of his tomb three days later! In the first two books of the series, we discussed the symmetries of said resurrections and the whole ego death-inducing commonalities regarding the DMT experience alongside the myth of Osiris; but could there be more to the myth of resurrection than meets the eye? The Great Pyramid of Giza is classically depicted as the burial place of kings, although rather bizarrely, there have never been any mummified remains found within these grandiose structures which continue to mystify the greatest minds in 21st-century thinking! Typically, the mainstream narrative defends their outdated dogma by simply stating that looters would have removed the riches and remains of the pharaoh long ago. Granted, this makes a little sense to an untrained eye, but why on earth would they construct such colossi for burial purposes when the vast majority of ancient royal dignitaries have already been found miles away from the Giza Plateau in the all too aptly named Valley of the Kings? There remains a somewhat unanswered conundrum regarding one particular king who wasn't buried within the confines of his tomb in the Valley of Kings. It would, however, make more sense that the pyramids were built to somewhat starve and stimulate the senses into a resurrection process whilst one was still actually alive! A verse from the Gospel of Philip is extremely revealing regarding this particular train of thought!

RESURRECTING REALITIES

Most are extremely aware of the notion of the *rising phoenix*; a wholly symbolic metaphor for the idea of immorality and rebirth from the ashes of what once was, but it is absolutely essential to first understand its ancient and allegorical origins. Greek mythology has somewhat championed the iconography of the phoenix. However, it is merely just another inherited cosmology from their Ancient Egyptian ancestry once again. The Ancient Egyptian's original deified avifauna of choice was the heron; an aquatic species that typically construct its nests amongst the reeds. This particular deity was recognized as the Bennu, a self-creating God of both creation and resurrection; and was therefore closely associated with the Ancient Egyptian God of Resurrection, and our old friend, Osiris! The name Bennu, however, is related to the Egyptian verb *'wbn'*, which is typified as translating to 'to rise in brilliance' and 'to shine'! Surely, it's not just merely coincidental once again to suggest the possibility of another unerring commonality in the face of resurrecting, reeds, shining and of course, Osiris – and dare I say it, DMT? The Bennu also adorns the cone-like headdress of Osiris, which we discovered in *Deities, Myth & tryptamines* was profoundly alike the photoreceptors within the human eye and the pineal gland; their fundamental functionality being loosely described as resurrecting consensus reality from within the scope of the electromagnetic spectrum. How many coincidences need to be stacked together before the word 'connection' is accepted? In *The Spirit in the Sky,* we uncovered the all too clear commonalities between Jesus and Osiris, a methodology that now appears to have come almost full circle. In the Bible, we learn, that baby Moses was discovered within the Ark of Bulrushes which is more commonly described as a bed of reeds. The Bible, however, also describes Jesus as the 'new Moses', and with good reason too. It's widely accepted that Jesus was known to be a Nazarene and the etymology of Nazareth is extremely revealing. The word is derived from Hebrew and is translated as both 'to watch', and 'shoot' or 'branch' (of a tree), but also as a 'reed'. Coincidently, or by design, Jesus is also spoken of in terms of the *Amen*, and in the Far East, Japan supports a creation cosmology by which their Supreme Being, Kunitotokotashi, is self-created via a reed shoot. Even more astonishing, we find, Kunitotokotashi's primordial consort in the creation of the universe is called (*Amen*)ominakanushi, no less! Returning to Ancient Mesopotamia, or more specifically, Ancient Sumer, there appear a great number of oddities regarding their own Tree of Life. Misunderstood for the last 5000 years or so, surviving Sumerian reliefs have caused a lot of controversy and speculation. Conspiracy theorists and ufologists have long decided that the iconography of the era depicts ancient aliens above the Tree of Life. Nothing's off the table here but I believe that said carvings are far more telling of the resurrection process, albeit the Bennu or phoenix's metamorphic ascension for higher spiritual or conscious awareness via the sacred secretion from within the Tree of Life! Incidentally, the Ancient Egyptian word for 'reed', considered the foremost plant, was 'aaru', which (as Laird Scranton points out) is comparable to the name of the foremost priest of the Dogon, known as the 'Arou' priest. In the phonetics of cosmology, 'ar' implies the coming or ascension of energy, while 'ru' implies the

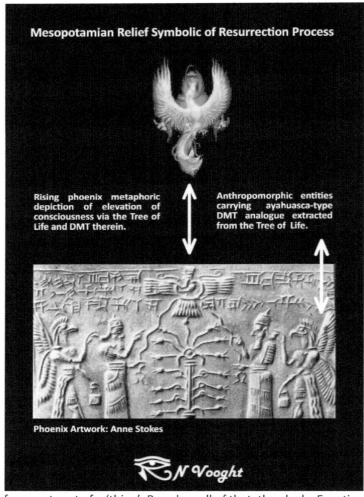

Mesopotamian Relief Symbolic of Resurrection Process

Rising phoenix metaphoric depiction of elevation of consciousness via the Tree of Life and DMT therein.

Anthropomorphic entities carrying ayahuasca-type DMT analogue extracted from the Tree of Life.

Phoenix Artwork: Anne Stokes

N Vooght

foremost part of a 'thing'. Based on all of that, the glyphs Egyptian word for 'reed' also reads, 'that which comes or ascends foremost'! Phoenix, indeed!

Fields of Aaru

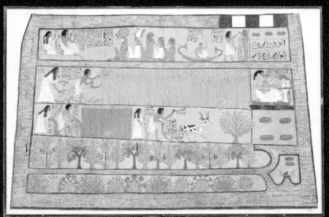

Above: Harvesting reeds in preparation for journeying into the Duat or 'otherworld'.

 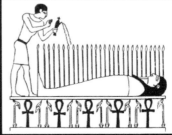

Above Left: Reed glyphs reading, 'That which ascends foremost'.
Above Right: Resurrection scene depicting reeds and the ankh symbology for the Key of Life.

Further to this, however, there also appears to be an undeniable etymological link between the notion of reeds and the Myth of Osiris. It is well documented that our God of Resurrection, Osiris, was dismembered into several parts which were scattered across the land before his wife and lover, Isis, methodically gathered Osiris' limbs in order for her to subsequently resurrect her husband once again. Ancient scripture suggests that Isis was successful in her endeavour to re-member her man, albeit without his manhood or phallus; something which would maybe suggest that those searching for a better understanding of this wholly metaphorical resurrection should continue to look for it. It is often stated that those of us who quest these ancient mysteries with intent; Seek, and ye shall find! And with context to this particular train of thought, there is a glaringly-apparent connection that has gone almost unnoticed until now. Why would the Ancient Egyptian 'underworld' be so specifically linked to a Field of Reeds? What's its significance? Well, one of the most common 'reeds' the globe-over, is recognized as the canary reed. This particular strain of reed is most often found in abundance scattered across marchlands and riverbanks just like our heron, Bennu bird, or indeed phoenix. The scientific name for this variety of reeds or grass is known as Phalaris Grass, or more specifically, Phalaris Arundinacea. For it is also more commonly known as the Shining Reed, which may also be a direct nod towards the Shining Followers of Horus or Aku Shemsu Hor of previous chapters! It is a well-documented and scientific fact that Phalaris Grass holds extractable potentials of the entheogenic compounds N, N DMT, 5-MeO DMT, and 5-OH-DMT (bufotenine), as well as Hordenine and 5-MeO NMT! It is also worth noting here that the mysterious Hindu elixir of immortality known only as

Soma, was said to have been extracted via a stone grinding technique which left a green stain upon the stones which were tasked with part of the extraction process from an otherwise unknown source. It is readily accepted that there were in all likelihood, several unidentified ingredients that went into the preparation of Soma. However, some of the more favoured candidates for psychedelic analogues just do not seem to fit the profile. Psilocybin, for example, doesn't tend to leave a green stain on the mortar which would see it ground upon. And, in my opinion, although sometimes seen as somewhat 'trippy' but certainly not worldview-shattering, cannabis undoubtedly holds a great deal of otherwise hidden healing potentials but must realistically be cast aside when considering a viable contender to what can surely only be a DMT-type analogue capable of altering one's perception of consensus reality.

It's not an easy task to tie these commonalities together in a coherent context because much of our history has been somewhat clouded by both time and text itself. There's a great number of other methodologies, which for the scope of this particular work, have been omitted for the sake of simplicity and publication purposes; however, there is one extremely eye-opening text which has otherwise been omitted from the Bible for purposes unknown – the Gospel of Philip. The Gospel of Philip is considered a Gnostic text which was compiled around the third century – in Egypt! For all intents and purposes, it rather specifically states that the notion of 'resurrection' is designed to be used as a device to reach the 'otherworld', albeit Heaven, and return again while the initiate is actually still alive! Fellow researcher and writer, Freddy Silva's *must-read* material, *The Lost Art of Resurrection*, didactically deep-dives into the realm of resurrection like no other. For, Silva reveals an age-old practice that has been preserved upon the walls of the so-called burial chamber of Tuthmose iii for the past 3500 years. Thutmose iii tomb, however, was actually discovered on the other side of the Valley of the Kings, which begs the question; why would a pharaoh need more than one burial site? And why indeed, would the empty burial chamber have access to a well – if, in fact, the pharaoh was presumed dead? Well, the answer is staggeringly obvious, as the pharaoh was clearly alive at the time of its use – its sole purpose being to prepare the pharaoh for the afterlife and beyond, by way of a shamanic initiation ceremony which is spoken of in great detail and via the accompanying hieroglyphic evidence which outlines a resurrection process for the living! The impressive high-relief carvings within the chamber depict the pharaoh touching his brow, symbolic of the third eye, in preparation for this sacred journey into the realms of the metaphysical. The word tomb is synonymous with 'womb', which is in itself somewhat revealing regarding the Ancient Egyptian train of thought. Its methodology wholly encompasses the notion of a living resurrection whereby the initiate would be seen to be roused from a womblike experience before being proclaimed 'raised from the dead'. The text inside the chamber itself is known today as the Treatise of the Hidden Chamber; a text which rather explicitly instructs the living initiation candidate on how to navigate the Fields of Aaru (Reeds) and return! It ostensibly states that 'It is good for the dead to have this knowledge, but also for the person who is on Earth…Whoever understands these mysterious images is a well-provided light being. Always a person can enter and leave the Otherworld. Always speaking to the living ones. Proven to be true a million times.' The ceremonial sarcophagus in the center of the tomb/womb was also

Classic Resurrection/Initiation Scenes From Abydos Depicting Osiris Very Much Alive & Well

ritually furbished, or indeed lined with reeds; another symbolic nod in the direction of the entheogenic compound (DMT) clearly utilized from within the reeds themselves, which would give direct access to the Duat/Otherworld! The text goes on to describe the newly resurrected candidate as being, 'transformed into a radiant spiritual being of illumination'; which would also appear to reflect the 21st-century psychonaut's mindset upon returning from a classical DMT breakthrough experience! It is now commonly accepted that DMT actually tricks the brain into a death-like state of mind before seemingly passing through the brain-blood barrier and leaving its user metaphorically resurrected thereafter! The much-suppressed Gospel of Philip rather categorically expresses these sentiments when stating; 'Those who say they will die first and then rise are in error. If they do not first receive the resurrection while they live, when they die, they will receive nothing.'

By way of believing in a literal and wholly-religious interpretation of the resurrection process, Silva states, 'that they are confusing a spiritual truth with an actual event', and that Philip himself goes on to describe fundamental Christianity as 'the faith of fools!'. The Bible dictates somewhat exponentially the teachings therein are almost completely allegorical in nature.

The concept of resurrecting while alive is also reflected in the writings of the Pyramid Texts. Utterance 213, the closest text to the so-called sarcophagus, couldn't be any more assuring when announcing, 'O Unas, you have not departed dead, you have departed alive to sit upon the throne of Osiris.' Something which David Elkington points out in his 2001 publication *The Ancient Language of Sacred Sound 'The Acoustic Science of the Divine'*, by rather eloquently elaborating upon the Ancient Greek etymolog of Osiris, by linguistically exposing us to the ever-present notion that the Christian tradition of the Resurrection of Jesus is, in fact, a resurrection of the tale of Osiris.

"Osiris is a Greek translation of the Egyptian 'Asar'. When Asar inherits the earthly kingdom, he is united with his heavenly father, Geb, so his name takes the original spellings of 'Giza', the others being Gesa and Gesu; the latter being an original spelling of Jesus. Giza represents the consummation of the sacred marriage between Gasar and Isis (Osiris and Isis), and the location where the two become one is in the bridal chamber, otherwise known as the King's Chamber of the Great Pyramid, that vast edifice and portal into the Otherworld."

Source: Richard Cassarro

SAME GIZA?

This particular chamber of initiation appears to permeate cultures the globe over; a rite of passage by which the practitioner would first consume a wholly psychedelic cocktail, the contents of which were known only to those who presided over the entire ceremony. The underlying reason for the consummation of such elixirs was to induce the initiate with a life-changing *near-death experience*, whereby the candidate would presumably disengage with consensus reality via an *out-of-body experience* before returning back to the physical with an apparent higher fundamental understanding of the nature of reality. Once this shamanic journey into the metaphysical was over, the initiate would rise from the sensory-depleting sarcophagus and tomb/womb and be pronounced 'raised from the dead', albeit resurrected! There are clues to the elixir's contents, however, should we care to read between the lines? For example, in Ancient Greece, the Mysteries of Eleusis rather decidedly speak in terms of the *kykeon*. The Goddess who presided over the Elysian Mystery Schools was Demeter, the Goddess of Agriculture. Demeter's traditional symbology gives us unparalleled insight into the nature of the kykeon and its death-state-inducing contents. Like most Gods and Goddesses of antiquity, Demeter is symbolic of a plethora of iconology which in this particular case includes wheat, barley, poppies, winged serpents, and the horn of plenty! The horn of plenty which was traditionally seen to be filled with ears of wheat which may well be likened to the Norse mythology of the Gjallarhorn and the well of knowledge beneath Yggdrasil, the Tree of Life. The notion of wheat being the source of the elixir in question arrives via the wholly-symbolic connotation alongside the colour purple. For it's the psychoactive substance ergot from which LSD is derived that appears as a purple-colored mold upon cereal crops such as wheat which may have thence been distilled into a consumable mind-altering and visionary cocktail. Broadly speaking, the story of Demeter rather decidedly describes her as a Goddess of both the Earth and the underworld alike. Let it also be known that the modern-day opiate, Opium, is extracted via the Goddess's go-to flora of choice, the poppy! The extraordinary commonalities regarding the Ancient Greek and Egyptian methodologies continue to astound because the goal of both Ancient Egyptian and Elysian Mysteries was to visit and thus return from the otherworld and declared 'risen'. We have already discovered that the Egyptian otherworld was described as the Duat or Fields of Aaru (reeds), but should it surprise us then to find that the destination for Greek initiates was known as the Elysian Fields? Fields of reeds, or indeed cereal, it doesn't really matter. What does matter, however, is the underlying fact that these entirely symbolic references appear to be frightfully obvious regarding the proverbial keys to the doors of the underworld! Having spent some thirteen years studying the mystery schools in Egypt, the celebrated philosopher extraordinaire, Plato, reveals his own first-hand experience in the resurrection process by revealing; "Those who are initiated into the great mysteries perceive a wondrous light. Purer regions are reached, and fields where there is singing dancing, sacred words, and divine visions, inspire holy awe. Then the man, perfected and initiated, free and able to move super-physically, without constraint, celebrates the mysterious with a crown on his head. He lives among pure men and saints. He sees on earth the many who have not yet been initiated or purified, buried in the darkness, and through fear of death, clinging to their ills for want of belief in the happiness of the beyond."

And, "We beheld the beautiful visions and were initiated into the mystery which may be truly called blessed."

And speaking of his journey into the abode of the Gods, Plato continues, "a reality with which true knowledge is concerned, a reality without colour or shape, intangible but utterly real, apprehensible only by the intellect which is the pilot of the soul."

Silva once again adds further weight to Plato's insight into the Mysteries of Eleusis by pointing out 'that the aim of the philosopher is to become conscious of the wisdom found only in the superphysical reality of the Otherworld while still living.'

A sentiment held in high regard by Plato once again; "True philosophers make dying their profession, and to them of all people death is least alarming...(for they are) glad to set out for the place where there is the prospect of attaining the object of their lifelong desire, which is Wisdom....If one is a real philosopher, one will be of the firm belief that one will never find Wisdom in all its purity in any other place."

Plato's by no means alone when regarding historical philosophers of the era. Themistius, also known as Euphrades, casually recalls; "At the point of death, the soul has the same experience as those who are being initiated into the great mysteries. At first, it wanders and wearily hurries to and fro, and journeys with suspicion through the dark like a person who is uninitiated; then come all the terrors before the final initiation, shuddering, trembling, sweating, amazement: then one is struck with a marvelous light, one is received into pure regions and meadows, with voices and dances and the majesty of holy sounds and shapes; among these, he who has fulfilled initiation wanders free, and released and bearing his crown joins in the divine communion, and consorts with pure and holy men."

Themistius continues, "There are initiatory rites, by means of which are revealed, not the mysteries of the municipal temple, but of the world itself, the vast temple of all the Gods...To be initiated is to experience the same knowledge as one obtains from death –

though of course, with initiation the seeker returns to this world and does not die!"

These quite remarkable extracts above would certainly ring true for almost every 21st-century psychonaut upon returning from the so-called DMT realm with new eyes in which to view this, and quite possibly, other existential realities otherwise hidden from our everyday ocular capacity!

Rather remarkably, at the time of writing this particular publication, I was struck by the most surreal synchronicity. To some, the first glance at our model of a psychedelic path into the mysteries of the Ancients may seem somewhat speculative. However, on the contrary, the evidence presented on 27th June 2022 by way of the highly respected *LiveScience* publishers, we encounter an extremely telling article headlined, '*Secret ancient Andean passageways may have been used in rituals involving psychedelics*'. The article goes on to describe how archaeologists uncovered a complex series of hidden passageways deep within the ancient Chavin de Huantar temple complex in the Peruvian Andes. It continues by outlining the current working hypothesis that the chambers were used in a religious capacity by incorporating psychedelics into their daily rituals. The temple chambers themselves are thought to have been constructed sometime between 3200 and 2200 years ago which is wholly (not holy) in accordance with what was happening across the Atlantic during the same period. Once again, and championing our own train of thought into psychedelic antiquity, the researchers revealed; "Some of the dark and isolated chambers may have been used for sensory deprivation, ritual visual or auditory and tactile disorientation."

Amongst the current excavations finds, they unearthed two large ritual bowls, one of them decorated with the symbolic head and wings of a condor, a large Andean bird of prey. It's widely believed that the Ancient Inca cosmology revered this sacred bird as they understood it to have been a communicator between the Upper World, Hana Pacha, and the earthly domain of Kay Pacha. Thus, the Inca deified the condor as a messenger between heaven and earth. Remember our phoenix from Ancient Greece? Further to the article, however, it goes on to speculate the similarities beneath the pyramids of Teotihuacan in central Mexico which also hold much in common with those of the Giza Plateau. Anthropologists have also put forward that the bowls may have been used as mortars whose initial function would have been to grind up potential psychedelic substances for religious ceremonies. Adding further weight to our argument, the archaeologists go as far as stating that the tradition in Chavin was to inhale hallucinogenic snuff, which was more than likely utilized from the seed pods of the vilca tree, which is considered rich in highly extractable potentials of DMT! Now, let's return to Mesopotamia and connect some dots and try to see the bigger picture. They say a picture can paint a thousand words, but what if it was capable of more? Far more. What if it was able to describe the nuts and bolts of the universe and the nature of reality?

It's here in our study into the nature of the Otherworld that we now turn our attention to what is today fondly termed as Sacred Geometry. So it is my intention, with the help of Plato and the Jewish/Hebrew tradition known as Merkabah and the Kabbalah, to navigate us back to our original line of inquiry – the Tree of Life.

MERKABAH

Much controversy surrounds the Ancient Egyptian philosophy of the spirit of the recently deceased. The spirit or soul of a person was defined by the notion of the *Ba* and *Ka*, a concept that appears to be integral to understanding the passage or journey into the afterlife, or indeed, the otherworld. The 'Ka' is described as being synonymous with the 'lifeforce' of the individual which is essentially attached to both the body and statuettes or idols that accompanied the body within the tomb or resting place. It was believed that the 'Ka' was still able to eat and drink as it watched over the body, but was unable, however, to leave the confines of the tomb itself. On the other hand, the 'Ba' was likened to the 'soul' of the dead which served as a connection between the realm of the living and the dead. It is largely understood that the 'Ba' was able to leave the tomb and traverse the realm of the dead. The combination of the lifeforce and soul was often referred to as the 'Akhu', which saw the transition of the recently parted in the afterlife. Interestingly, the 'akhu' which is somewhat loosely translated as 'light' or 'shining', is the suffix of the ancient archaeological site of Tiwanaku in Bolivia – home of the much-famed Gateway of the Sun, which shares remarkable commonalities with construction techniques witnessed at the Osirion in Abydos, Egypt! Even more revealing, is the etymology of the place itself; Tiwanaku translates as 'Place of the Shining Ones', no less! Once the Ba and Ka were untied upon death and became the 'akhu', the 'akhu' was then considered to become immortal via the 'Sahu'. The 'Sahu' however, was personified as the now spiritualized 'incorruptible soul' and free to loose itself amongst the abode of the Gods and the imperishable stars above. Rather remarkably, we identified Sahu in *Deities, Myth & Tryptamines* via

the constellation of Orion as the 'hidden one'. This all-encompassing constellation we have found is uncannily alike the molecular structure of DMT – which itself has been more often than not, recalled as the abode of the Gods! There does remain a common, if not hidden, link here regarding the conceptual design of the pyramids seen as tombs, resurrection, shining creator Gods, the molecular structure of DMT, and the allegorical nature of the Tree of Life! Now, there is an ancient oddity that Egyptologists have fondly familiarised the world with called the Bent Pyramid. Typically accredited to the pharaoh Sneferu sometime around 2600 BC, the pyramid itself is composed of what appears to be two separate parts, albeit, levels of construction. The mainstream mindset will of course point out that the architects had not foreseen the problematic angle of incline within the base layer of the pyramid's original dimensions; that the elevation was too much of a strain on the cumbersome blocks to be able to support the entire edifice should they continue; that they, therefore, re-evaluated its design preferring a much lesser gradient before reaching its eventual apex. This particular train of thought makes a great deal of sense, nevertheless, there does emerge another altogether more profound and indeed preordained plan to the otherwise mystifying makeup of this rather peculiar pyramid. All things considered, the Ancient Egyptians rarely, if at all, made mistakes when constructing such megalithic marvels the likes of which are witnessed upon the Giza Plateau. So why would we assume that this was the case here? Firstly, Sneferu, translates as the 'Shining One', another oddity in itself, for as we have already seen, the 'shining ones' were far from capable of making such colossus mistakes! Secondly, the 'shining ones' were considered Creator Gods throughout Ancient Egyptian mythology which would certainly suggest that this preferred building blueprint was actually 'meant to be! Moreover, as Freddy Silva eloquently articulates in his publication *The Divine Blueprint*, the actual deviating angles of incline reveal an absolute wealth of understanding should we care to look. The initial course of blocks dictates an angular rise which is characteristic of that which is fundamental to the geometric proportions of the hexagon, just as the upper slope rises at an angle ostensibly fundamental to the appearance of a pentagon. Here then, the otherwise irregular angular slopes of the Bent Pyramid appear to reflect the integral angular structure of the building blocks of life. From essential amino acids such as tryptophan (from which the formulaic structure of DMT is derived) to the molecular structure of our very own DNA, this basic template is fundamental to life as we know it! The extreme profundity of such correlations is largely overlooked, if not simply ignored, by those who control the historical narrative. But should they care to read between the lines of the all-too-clear allegorical nature of the ancients, something inexplicitly ironic begins to appear! For, as we have witnessed so far during our deep dive into antiquity, there's an obvious and overriding sense of understanding between the otherwise divided trains of thought regarding religions, didactic art, and the perplexing possibility that pyramids might serve to unite humanity as a whole. For instance, many of the world's popular religions have more often than not, drawn upon the esoteric understandings of the Ancient Egyptians. The artisans of Ancient Egypt themselves were much-famed for producing artwork and pyramids alike. However, it's somewhat of an oddity that there is no artwork within the Great Pyramid, and

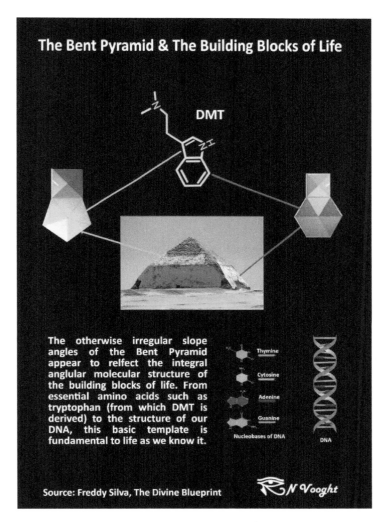

The Bent Pyramid & The Building Blocks of Life

DMT

The otherwise irregular slope angles of the Bent Pyramid appear to relfect the integral anglular molecular structure of the building blocks of life. From essential amino acids such as tryptophan (from which DMT is derived) to the structure of our DNA, this basic template is fundamental to life as we know it.

Thymine
Cytosine
Adenine
Guanine
Nucleobases of DNA

DNA

Source: Freddy Silva, The Divine Blueprint

RN Vooght

there are no pyramids within the content of their collective works of art. One would assume that the builders of such a marvelous feat of engineering would in fact celebrate such a success and incorporate it somehow into at least one piece for the prosperity of their ingenuity. But there's simply nothing! Egyptologists dismiss this by way of pointing to the only surviving papyrus which relies upon the word of a sailor's inventory which speaks of transporting several blocks to the Giza Plateau via the river Nile. Granted, this actually happened. But the context to which it clearly refers appears to be far more of a refurbishment project instead of the now preposterously accepted complete construction of this awe-inspiring colossus. Simply put, they have nothing else to offer! A tomb, they say. Well, they might inadvertently be on to something; but not in the traditional way of thinking.

With everything we've learned thus far, is it too much to take for rational thinking to consider the Great Pyramid as being a form of transcendental transportation for the conscious mind to traverse the cosmos and commune with the immaterial 'other' and beyond? One of the oldest and most sacred teachings that have survived the tides of time is the Torah. The Torah, being the first five books of the Hebrew Bible, an offshoot of which is described as the Kabbalah; is an oral tradition regarding the nature of God, the infinite, the finite, and the universe. In the first two books of the series, we discovered that it was the word of God that created the *universe*; the etymology of which decidedly defined *uni* as 'one' and *verse* meaning 'word' or 'song'. The metaphor here is that the birth of the universe was and is born out of vibration, albeit resonance. Further to our discovery, we learned that the Bible's principal message was that *God is Light*. This is something that the Torah and Judaism naturally agree with. For when it speaks of the Tribe of Judah, it recalls them as being a 'light unto

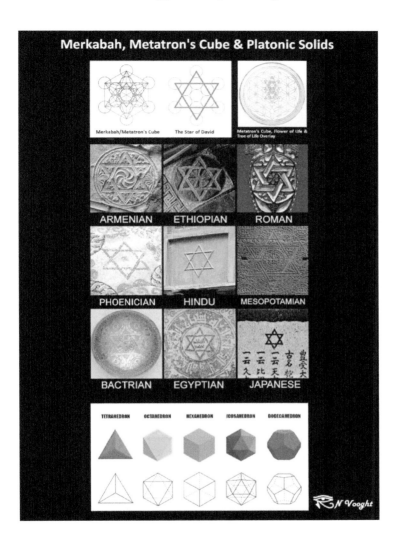

the nations' and that the Tribe of Judah were encamped upon the Eastern horizon (the point of the rising sun/son). *And*, that they were 186,400 in number. It's here where you will recall the distance in miles that light travels within a vacuum; 186,400mps! Lots to ponder indeed. But returning to the Ancient Egyptian concept of the Ka (soul) and Ba (spirit) *and* the possible functionality of the Great Pyramid – is there any clear and common ground regarding the oral traditions of the Kabbalah? You bet there is! Kabbalah is also spoken of in terms of the Merkabah, which is centered upon the visions of Ezekiel who prophesized stories concerning the ascension to heavenly palaces and the throne of God. The word Merkabah itself translates directly as 'thing to ride in', also synonymous with a 'chariot' is which mentioned forty-four times in the text. Ezekiel goes as far as describing said 'chariots' as comprising of having wheels within wheels and bearing 'beings' of 'living creatures' with wings – with the heads of a man, lion, ox, and eagle. An oddity in the extreme; for those unfamiliar with the realm of sentient beings witnessed via the DMT experience, that is! Ezekiel goes on to describe an unbuilt temple (presumably of the mind), the likes of which was built in Jerusalem and is described as the Temple of Solomon – father to David, who constructed a second temple upon the same site. It is the same site whereupon Jacob witnessed the face of God. It is the same site that Jacob came to name Peniel. The same site by which we measured the distance between Gobekli Tepe/Port Asar (Umbilical of Osiris) and the Osirion. The same site which our imaginary umbilical passed over (Jewish traditions Pass Over representing the redemption of humanity via the death and subsequent *resurrection* of Jesus/Gasar/Gesa/Giza). Nothing to see here! Well, of course, there is. If we're correct in postulating that the Great Pyramid was, amongst other things, used as a vehicle that enabled the *Spirit* or *Ka* of an individual to loose the bonds of the body in order to traverse the immaterial realm of the 'other' or underworld, then there must be some kind of etymological connection regarding its painstakingly perplexing functionality. As we have already seen, the linguistical evidence undoubtedly ties a great deal of popular world religions to an Ancient Egyptian origin, and the teachings of the Kabbalah are almost certainly guilty of doing so too. The Ancient Egyptian word for 'pyramid' is generally accepted as being described as 'mr', whereby there were no vowels used to accentuate the spoken word at the time. It is here where the use of linguistics is incorporated by way of inserting the vowel in order to articulate its direct translation in the modern era. And in doing so, we arrive at the word *Mer*, meaning 'pyramid'. If we endeavour to take it one step further by somewhat logically adding the notion of the *Spirit* (Ka) and the *Soul* (Ba) into the equation, something profoundly revealing begins to emerge. *Mer-Ka-Ba! Something to ride in, indeed!* Even more astounding, however, we find that the traditional Merkabah is spoken of in terms of the Tree of Life, the sacred geometry of which has been illustrated to clearly define its all-encompassing methodology – something that was also evident amongst the Ancient Egyptian counter-culture the Assyrians. By overlaying the Merkabah's Tree of Life with that of the Assyrians of Ancient Sumer, the picture begins to get a lot clearer. The winged deities which hold much in common with the prophetic visions beheld by Ezekiel, appear to be nurturing or harvesting it. Interestingly, these winged beings also appear holding pine cones symbolic of the Pineal/Peniel gland and buckets which are commonly used to contain ayahuasca-type analogues during shamanic ceremonies from the South American

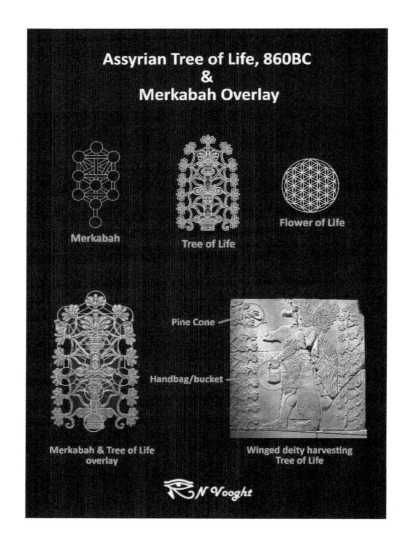

Assyrian Tree of Life, 860BC
&
Merkabah Overlay

Merkabah

Tree of Life

Flower of Life

Pine Cone

Handbag/bucket

Merkabah & Tree of Life overlay

Winged deity harvesting Tree of Life

Andes to the mystical rites of the Elysian Mystery Schools of Ancient Greece! The evidence here is overwhelming from Pre-Colombian, Peru, to Plato himself! Now, by way of coming full circle regarding this ancient ayahuasca-like analogue imbibed by those of the initiatory mystery schools for the sake of 'resurrecting' their outlook upon the mundane materialistic mechanics of everyday waking reality; we need to look no further than 21st-century science, and indeed, sacred geometry to gain the very same psychedelic insight into the nuts and bolts of the world(s) which is (or are) evidently all around us!

Luke 17:21

"The Kingdom of God is within you!"

As is the God-inducing sap, seed, or indeed, reed that enables us to witness this ourselves first-hand; DMT!

SACRED GEOMETRY & THE TREE OF LIFE

The all-encompassing ancient axiom *Sacred Geometry* refers to the universal understanding of both the sacred (meaning connected to God and deserving of veneration) and the omnipotent numbers or mathematical connections derived from the measurements of planet earth ('geo' meaning 'earth' and 'metry' meaning 'to measure'). No matter how infinitely small or indeed grandiose, the mathematical proportions extracted from this universal constant are always present and absolute. They can be witnessed from measurements attained from subatomic molecular structures within the microscopic all the way through to the birthing of stars and the theorized shape and structure of the universe itself!

Sacred Geometry, however, is not strictly considered a new-age ideology. Far from it. Most of what we deem to understand today had been meticulously documented within the proportions of ancient structures such as the Great Pyramid and temple constructions across the globe. Our ancient ancestry, it would appear, was privy to a far more universal understanding than 21st-century scholars would care to believe. Before we endeavour to dissect this unfathomable appreciation clearly incorporated by our predecessors of planet earth, it is essential for us to comprehend where it all began. And there's no better place to start than with the Big Bang. It is here where I would like to extract some of the narratives from the highly-recommended resource that is YouTubes *After Skool* presentation entitled 'The Story of Creation Through Sacred Geometry'. Mark Wooding's extremely eloquent and thought-provoking video is, in my opinion, the most comprehensive and engaging 'masterpiece' on the subject of Sacred Geometry found anywhere online! This extremely thought-provoking video short delivers probably the best-illustrated understanding of the somewhat blurry lines between the notion of something, nothing, and everything – which in itself can be derived from the so-called sacred number 108!

108

1 = One Thing (Something)
0 = No Thing (Nothing)
8 = Everything (Infinity)

In the early 20th century, a Belgian priest named Georges Lemaitre introduced the Big Bang Theory, from which he went on to theorize that the universe began from a single primordial atom. The idea received a major boost from Edwin Hubble's observation that galaxies across the cosmos were speeding away from us in all directions. But where did the Big Bang come from? What happened before the Big Bang which occurred around 13.8 billion years ago? Someday we might know the answer, and once we have the answer, the next logical question will be; what came before that? Well, sacred geometry reverse engineers our method of scientific exploration and it does so by starting with the logical beginning of everything, which, before there was something – there was nothing. The universe was without form and void. And darkness was upon the face of the deep. The first thing to come into existence was a point; before anything could or indeed can be, it has to start with a point. A point has no space, it has no dimensions as it's so small that it can't be measured. Yet, it encompasses everything within it. There is no particular name for this point however, for the purposes of our own exploration, we shall (like many religious trains of thought) call this point, *Spirit*!

And what is the first thing *spirit* does? It becomes conscious. It becomes aware. 360 degrees of awareness in the vast emptiness of the void. The Ancient Egyptians believed that this innate aspect of consciousness is what sparked the process of creation. Then, what did *Spirit* do? The only thing it could do! It moved! The first three lines of Genesis in the Bible; In the beginning, God created the Heaven and the Earth. We learned through the second book in the series that the so-called Creation process as recorded in the Bible is linked directly to the Divine Proportion, or Golden Ratio via the much-heralded Fibonacci sequence of numbers. The understanding being that the first three days of Creation are cited in verses 5, 8, and 13. These numbers, we found, were also pivotal in the 'creation' of the Great Pyramid of Egypt which is believed to have once stood at a height of 5,813 inches. Furthermore, we discovered that a circle with a radius of 5,813 inches has a circumference of 36,524 inches, which correlates rather comfortably alongside the accepted number of days in a solar year at 365.24 days! A beautifully elemental yet scientifically acceptable standpoint that was built into the proportions of the Great Pyramid from the geometry of a simple circle. However, the Earth was still without form and void, and darkness was upon the face of the deep, and the *Spirit* of God moved upon the face of the waters, and God said; 'Let there be Light.' 'God is Light' is the Bible's fundamental message. And so, there was Light. Now, interpretations of the Bible have varied a lot over time but the important thing to note here is that movement happened before there was Light. From the vantage of pure physics or mathematics motion is impossible in a void, you simply can't go anywhere, or fall, or rotate, there's just infinite emptiness in all directions – nothing but space! So, in order to move you need something in relation to move to. Before there was Light, there was movement and once *Spirit* created a point in space it was able to move the edge of its awareness and thus expand its conscious awareness, thereby creating another circle to form the vesica piscis. It is from this geometric blueprint from which the much-famed Ichthys, or Jesus Fish iconography is formed which is typically used to display one's affiliation to the Christian faith. The eye-shaped opening in the middle is the geometric image through which Light was created and it is also the geometric shape through which our eyes receive Light. *Spirit,* however, would continue to expand its awareness following the genesis pattern by moving to each intersection of the circumferences and expanding. The second movement creates the third circle which forms the Holy Trinity. With each movement, more information unfolds, and by the fourth motion, we have moved halfway around the first circle 180 degrees from the first motion. On the fourth day of Genesis, exactly half of creation was completed. After six movements (six days) a geometric miracle takes place; we have a complete pattern – the seed of life. This complete pattern is called the seed of life because it contains the recipe for life and all its potential within this particular three-dimensional realm of reality. The Ancients understood that the second rotation of circles forms a three-dimensional shape and called this cluster of spheres the Egg of Life. Our entire existence is dependent upon the Egg of Life structure. Everything about you, from your height to your eye colour was created through the Egg of Life form. *Spirit* would continue this pattern with a third rotation completing nineteen circles producing the Flower of Life; a shape that we have found throughout ancient cultures across the globe which appears to be somewhat amplified during a so-called 'threshold DMT experience'. And when the Flower of Life is extended out and all the circles are completed, the Fruit of Life is revealed! This is the sacred secret. Out of the Flower of Life

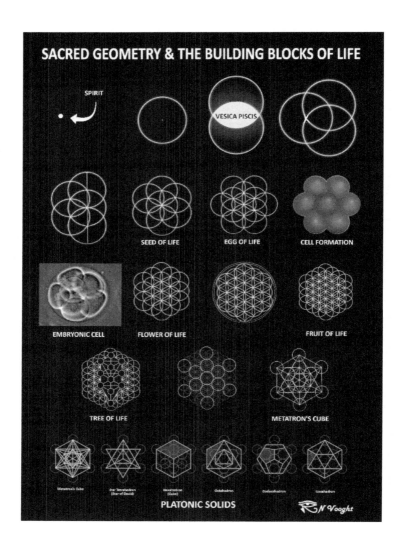

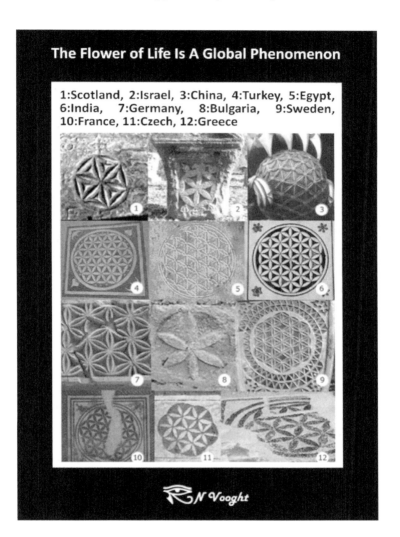

The Flower of Life Is A Global Phenomenon

1:Scotland, 2:Israel, 3:China, 4:Turkey, 5:Egypt, 6:India, 7:Germany, 8:Bulgaria, 9:Sweden, 10:France, 11:Czech, 12:Greece

RN Vooght

comes the Fruit, and the curved lines of the fruit are an entirely feminine shape. They represent formlessness and emotion. Once we add masculine energy or lines the formlessness begins to take shape and create what is described as Metatron's Cube! Metatron's Cube basically contains the fabric of reality, because out of this very particular shape we create the Platonic Solids. And with what we have learned from Plato's all-too-obvious descent into the higher-dimensional nature of the Elysian Mysteries, you can't help but wonder what this giant of geometric principles retained from his journeys into the DMT/LSD-infused initiations! Platonic solids, we find, have faces that are all the same size, edges that are all the same length, and angles that are all the same degree. And if put into a sphere, all the points will touch the edge of the sphere. These shapes were studied in ancient times by the Egyptians which in time was inherited by the Greeks, where Pythagoras would study them, and later Plato – which is where the name Platonic Solids originates. In all, there are only five Platonic solids, the cube, the tetrahedron, the octahedron, the icosahedron, and the pentagonal dodecahedron. Moreover, these geometric shapes are looked upon as the elemental forces of nature; Earth, Air, Fire, Water, and Ether. Every element in the Periodic Table has a geometric relation to one of the Platonic Solids. From the motion of atoms to molecules to viruses, to snowflakes and the shape of sound to the orbits of planets in our solar system – everything stems from this basic geometric information system and it all starts with a point; consciousness, albeit *Spirit*! Looking at ancient myths and religious teachings in a metaphorical sense as we have learned to do throughout our study together, and less in a 21st-century materialistic sense, allows us to decipher the encoded wisdom and may perhaps serve to unite the all-too-clear divide between science and *Spirit*. As Above So Below. There is as much greater than us as there is lesser than us. There is as much outside of us as there is inside us. Everything above us and everything below us is constructed from the same geometric proportions and relationships which manifest from a single point. When we study sacred geometry, we begin to understand our place in the universe. All this expansion of consciousness, all this curious exploration is really about is finding out who or indeed what we are! We are a mystery to ourselves, and to uncover where we came from has to be the deepest level of understanding from a human perspective. Everything from the smallest particle to the biggest star is connected, and we and DMT are at the absolute center of it all!

REED BETWEEN THE LINES

With reference to the DMT experience and the notion of 'contact' between ourselves and the possibility of an entirely real and observable entity-rich alien environment, and regardless of your particular stance upon the subject of UFOs, albeit UAPs (Unidentified Ariel Phenomena), there may soon prove to be a common thread for us to pull upon. Moreover, the otherwise unexplainable pretense for an interdimensional realm of sentient beings or entities which has become much-famed via the DMT breakthrough experience, might one day reveal a plethora of potential planetary portals known to the Ancients by which a means of direct contact may in fat be made! Sounds crazy, right? Well, nothing's off the table here and the science is seemingly in support of such a dramatic and somewhat insane statement. As we have seen throughout our study, the Ancients were privy to a wealth of scientific understanding which still appears to be some way ahead of our own here in the 21st century. In *The Spirit in the Sky,* we looked into the subatomic realms of exploration expressed via an ancient pictogram system employed by the ancient yet modern-day nomadic tribe of the Dogon. The Dogon's outlook upon the cosmology of the universe was strikingly similar to that of a physicist in the modern era. As we have seen via the ongoing works of fellow researcher and linguist Laird Scranton, the Dogon remain steadfast in the notion of a dual-cosmology which in effect explains the interaction between our physical domain and that of a twin and immaterial 'other' universe which are somewhat co-dependent upon one another regarding their existence. Scranton goes on to expertly explain the potentiality of such a thesis alongside the scientific world of exploration of the microcosmic and macrocosmic nature of our very existence. Today, this particular train of thought is described as Duality Theory, whereby the universe consists of two equal opposite halves, which are related by overlapping Galileian coordinates; which have exactly the opposite matters, energies, masses, motions, accelerations, and gravities. This in itself goes some way towards explaining the bizarre and inexplicable interaction between entangled subatomic photons of light behaving as 'one' regardless of the limitless distance between the two potentials which may be on opposite sides of the cosmos. Scranton elaborates upon this in his 2020 publication, *Primal Wisdom of the Ancients 'The Cosmological Plan For Humanity'*.

Scranton; "...the root philosophies of the archaic Samkhya cosmological tradition, where our universe is understood to be paired with a second, sibling universe. The Dogon share Samkhya's outlook that universes form in pairs. The view is that a flow of energy, essential to the life of both universes, scrolls cyclically between them. This energy carries potential mass along with it and so fosters a dynamic in which one universe grows progressively more massive while the other sees a corresponding reduction in mass, somewhat like the effect of sand moving through an hourglass. At the full extent of the cycle, this exchange of energy and mass culminates in what we perceive as a fully material one. However, Einstein's view of relativity insists that the time frame of an object (or a universe) must slow down as its mass increases, so therefore must also quicken as its mass decreases. Consequently, any virtually nonmaterial universe must persist within a much quicker time frame than the one that we experience. In the context of that quickened time frame, from the perspective of an outside observer, all events might seemingly occur at once. We might also see this quickened time frame as comparable to a state of quantum entanglement, where the quantum attributes of two or more particles (such as electrons) can be induced to behave as if they were effectively one particle, without regard to any apparent distance that separates them. An entire universe with its mass minimalized to this state of entanglement would outwardly appear as a single unified force, akin to the concept of Unity that defines non-materiality in many ancient traditions. The overall cycle of energy that scrolls between the two universes coincide with what the Buddhists refer to as the Yuga Cycle or Great Year. The implication is that, as a by-product of the differing time frames of the two universes, an ongoing shift occurs in humanity's ability to perceive its nonmaterial twin. In Hinduism and Buddhism, the domain of decreasing mass is known as the ascending universe, while the realm where the mass increases are known as the decreasing universe. Another important implication of this energy flow is that, during the intermediate periods of the cycle, the time frame and relative masses of the two universes must roughly equalize. At this point of parity, it might become thinkable to cross between the universes in much the same way that an airlock makes it possible for humans to transfer between regions of differing pressure. An airlock in a submarine or spacecraft effectively allows us to equalize inside and outside pressures and so facilitates safe movement into or out of the vessel."

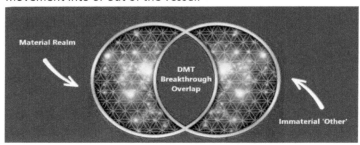

Another, if not simpler way to picture this is via the universal language via sacred geometry once again sees the overlapping spheres of the vesica piscis.

As you may recall from the earlier publications of this series of books, we learned of the almost identical cosmologies of the Buddhist tradition and that of the Dogon. And when explaining the outlooks of their insight into the nature of their unparalleled cosmologies the Buddhist tradition dictated that their insight was imparted to them via a nonhuman source. However, the Dogon went one step further by recalling that their own cosmology was imparted via a nonmaterial source which might now account for a wholly-intelligent overlap between the occupants of both the physical and nonmaterial universe; the nonmaterial other being such that it could possibly go some way towards explaining the all-too-real interdimensional connect between ourselves and the immaterial realm of the aforementioned DMT entities.

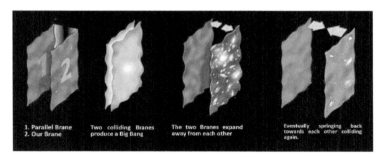

1. Parallel Brane
2. Our Brane

Two colliding Branes produce a Big Bang

The two Branes expand away from each other

Eventually springing back towards each other colliding again.

This entire thesis can also be somewhat better explained via the rapidly evolving hypothesis known today as Brane Theory. Brane theory is likened to String Theory and related theories such as Supergravity theories, whereby the concept of a Brane is described as a physical object which generalizes the notion of a point particle to higher dimensions of reality. Branes are typically exposed as dynamical objects which can propagate through spacetime according to the laws and rules of quantum mechanics. Furthermore, it is suggested that a Brane may utilize the four space-time dimensions of the universe which effectively make up its surface in a higher-dimensional space-time called the Bulk. The Bulk itself would appear somewhat invisible to our notion of three-dimensional reality but expanding nonetheless. It has also been put forward that this higher-dimensional Bulk may in fact overlap our own three-dimensional material reality somewhat akin to the Dogon cosmology referred to above. Here then, this in effect could produce the appearance of an otherwise invisible array of immaterial or indeed, otherworldly 'others' which fundamentally coexist beside us but beyond the scope or tools of everyday ocular perception. This in itself is better expressed via the nature of a lower two-dimensional plane of existence, whereby its interaction within the time frame of a three-dimensional reality or object overlapping or passing through it would appear beyond the scope of comprehension. For example, if a spherical (three-dimensional) object were to pass through a two-dimensional space or reality, the sphere itself could only be described as an expanding circle from a single point which increases to the circumference of the sphere before reducing down to a single point before disappearing once again. And it's here where I'd like to postulate the following conclusion to the observations made above. Once again, we find, the Dogon and Buddhist traditions appear to be in possession of a wealth of archaic understanding which can surely only be explained via a highly advanced albeit forgotten chapter of the human story where modern-day science is seemingly still playing catch-up. On the face of it, and as we have witnessed thus far in our observations of the Ancients, there are a great number of 'otherworldly' oddities which would seemingly defy explanation. From the myth of Osiris resurrecting alternate realities and the entity-rich 'underworld' of the Duat, the inexplicably familiar iconography of the deified Pre-Columbian artifacts which undoubtedly depict the higher-dimensional characteristics of the so-called DMT machine elves and entities, to the interaction between the physics-defying accounts of the UFO/UAP phenomenon, there may be a whole new world of exploration waiting for us to re-discover it. They certainly know more about us than we do of 'them'. And with the latest pictures direct from the James Webb Space Telescope shot from some 5 billion lightyears away from us, it is becoming ever-increasingly unlikely that we're alone in the vastness of the ever-expanding universe. I'm almost certain that several first-hand eye-witness accounts of UFO/UAPs are fundamentally material in nature and that their apparent appearance and presence here on planet earth is very much real. However, it now appears highly likely that a great deal of so-called sightings and indeed abductions may be accounted for via the overlapping time frames of this aforementioned cycle of twin universes interacting with one another. And rather ironically, the endogenous nature of the natural phenomenon known as DMT which permeates the planet, may one day play a key role in revealing the otherwise invisible and immaterial 'others' who co-habit the cosmos with and indeed the planet, alongside us.

In conclusion to our descent into antiquity, several otherwise anomalous ancient oddities have begun to paint a far clearer picture of the prehistoric appreciation for psychedelic substances from which the ever-apparent religious ideologies have been handed down to us. As we have seen, and for good reason, the original and most ancient axiom regarding the notion of resurrection arrives via the myth of Osiris. An allegorical account of a hero's journey which appears to have been restyled, reworked, rewritten, and remembered by almost every civilized culture across the face of the planet over the last 5000 years or more. From the tamarisk in Ancient Egypt, the Yew of Norse mythology, the Ceiba of Mayan tradition to the Tree of Awakening or Bodhi Tree of Buddhism; the entheogenic properties of DMT therein appear to be at the all-encompassing root of a religious well of reckoning recalling the notion of 'resurrection'. And as we have witnessed via the highly regarded words of Plato himself, the capacity to 'resurrect' one's soul or spirit from an entheogenic initiation ceremony entrusted to the selected few, was a sacred right of passage that could, and indeed should, be walked by those of us within the realm of the living and was by no means strictly limited to the fantastical follies of the outdated dogmas of religious ideologies. And so, I postulate that the Ancient Greek, Egyptian, Mesoamerican, South American, Aboriginal, Japanese, Norse, Assyrian, Christian, Islamic, Hindu, Buddhist, and Hebrew accounts of a heavenly bardo known as Elysium and the Fields of Aaru all stem from the ever-present pretences of a single 'reed' and the DMT therein. The traces of which appear to permeate prehistory and the planet alike. The crux of the matter remains. History and that of the human story are far older and more complicated than we are currently aware of. There was clearly a global and wholly-interconnected relationship with almost every archaic culture who have preserved the essence of the same story for millennia. I believe that drinking from Mimir, Kykeon, Soma, Ayahuasca, and the acacia or Lifeblood of Osiris are all essentially the same thing – the elixir of life and the key to the concept of immortality in an otherwise finite existence! Not that you live this life forever like some kind of vampire through the ages, but with a fundamental understanding that once this life's up it's not just simply faced to black. There's more. Surely, if consciousness arises out of the metaphysical and not just some kind of organic and compartmentalized brain reflex, and consciousness itself is more easily expressed as a flow state of energy instead – what could be more fulfilling? Science states that energy converts from one form to another – it doesn't die, it simply changes. Therefore, the same can be said of the conscious mind. It changes state. It flows. It simply moves on. I believe that the allegorical nature of all the sophisticated societies mentioned above was in fact in agreement regarding the otherworldly properties of DMT which seemingly gives us a whistle-stop tour of the cosmos from the micro to the macro and back again; all of which can be accessed via the common reed and acacia whilst we're still very much alive. And don't get me wrong here either, for it's certainly not a walk in the park. DMT, as we have learned is wholly responsible for momentarily tricking the brain into a death-like state of mind – and it's absolutely terrifying! You actually think you're dying. You feel yourself losing grip on your very existence. You begin to melt into the very fabric of your surroundings as your perception of reality is completely distorted by the fractal-like geometry of the information your brain is vying to compute. Then the fear just bursts like a bubble. You're no longer human. You see the flower of life. It's everywhere. You've left the material bonds of the body and been systematically launched into the unknowable. The infinite. You become one with the source. Maybe you died for real? You no longer care. You see the true nature of reality for what it is and you're comforted by the fact that life, or indeed Spirit, goes on! A kaleidoscopic chrysanthemum of crystalline clarity which is impossible to comprehend and keep. Although the familiarity of it all is absolutely astonishing. It's mesmeric. And 'they' know it's too much for you, but these entities just want you to watch — just like Jesus said. Watch! The kingdom is God is within you. It's everywhere. Then, pop! It's gone. You're alive. Back from the dead. Back from a metaphysical mindscape that completely over-rode your senses and you're adjusting to the seemingly odd-fitting meat suit you were wearing before you died moments before. Yes, you've been Resurrected! Your fear of death is extinguished. Your original outlook on reality forever shifted. Your heart feels lighter. Your soul feels upwardly raised. You have new eyes. You're enriched with a sense of love and compassion for the planet and everyone else on it. Spaceship Earth though is vulnerable. She spoke with you. She loves you. But more importantly, Gaia needs us to love her too!

RN VOOGHT

Please leave a review!

It means 'otherworlds' to me!

That's the Spirit...

RN

Graham Hancock:

"As the Consciousness Revolution unfolds, a web of patterns, connections and influences in the human story are being revealed. RN Vooght's research reintroduces us to omnipresent Osiris, the divinity immanent in humanity."

The Spirit in the Sky untangles the scientifically profound mythology surrounding Ancient Egyptian God of Resurrection, Osiris. Osiris is traditionally depicted as the celestial hunter of the heavens who is immortalised on a macrocosmic scale as the constellation of Orion. Osiris however, is also considered as the complete embodiment of 'all things acacia' - an ethnobotanical variety known for highly extractable potentials of the world's most illicit God-inducing psychoactive entheogen compound; which is also produced in the human brain. Famously dubbed 'The Spirit Molecule', N-N dimethyltryptamine also known as DMT, is a key ingredient of an ancient Amazonian shamanic tool called Ayahuasca and is described as the 'Vine of Souls'. Indeed, God is Di-vine. Moreover, the molecular structure or microscopic fingerprint of this nirvana-like state ofGod-induced perception is also a comprehensive'match' for the constellation of Orion! Have our ancient ancestors from an epoch forgotten methodically inserted a scientifically viable explanation to the riddle of human consciousness onto the cosmos? Is there a macroscopic mirror of the molecular structure of the Tree of Life hiding in plain sight? Furthermore, could the Egypt-illogical ideal fundamentally be supporting a battle-weary blueprint for all world religion? The Spirit in the Sky offers a 21st translation of the ancient and esoteric adage 'As Above So Below...'

Available via Amazon

Reviews

Spirit in the Sky is one of those books you will never forget reading, and will return to often. Exceptionally well written & beautifully illustrated, this book makes for riveting & easy reading of what are complex subjects: our Past, our Stars, our Beliefs & our Consciousness. As each page is turned, one can't help feel that you are most certainly reading what we, a species with amnesia, all once knew to be true - As Above, So Below. It makes absolute, brilliant sense. RN firmly deserves a position in the firmament of top cosmological & Egypta-LOGICAL researchers. I couldn't put it down.

Sandi, UK

Sci-fi or Sci-non-fi? An interesting introduction to the all too coincidental links between our unwritten history, spiritual awareness and the cosmos. The author presents expert evidence to support his theory of how the Gods are amongst us and exactly how you can discover them. A real third-eye opener! I look forwards to the next installment....if we're all still here.

Nick, UK

This book is critical to our current look at a new paradigm for us as a species. The author was clever in that he delivered thought provoking material that deeply questions the outdated paradigms of the past concerning Egypt. The mention of Atlantis and the history of Earths records was a welcome addition. Loved the Dogan chapter as having read similar material found it highlighted fascinating new material. A welcome addition to our Institutes Library! Best of Luck & Looking forward to more!

Darrelle, USA

First heard the author being interviewed on a podcast, he has his facts together along with quoting his sources plus researchers. I listened to a few more interviews along with reviews of his work. Comes across as very humble with his focus being on that the information is shared and not forgotten. You can see on social media/interviews he is up to discuss his work and interact with readers etc. The book's language is kept plane and simple so that it is accessible to all, along with the page layout which is very clear to read with a good number of colour images depicting the topics mentioned. The bibliography is detailed naming authors/researcher/books/website links.
You can think of this as three sectioned book in my opinion:
1) Deals with geography features formed by destructive events thousands of years ago, explaining why they are not say simple erosion features created over many years. Architectural feats we still have little understanding to how they were achieved.
2) Ancient civilisations and their relationship to the constellations encoding their information into stories that became mythology.
3) Discussion of DMT how the Egyptians left clues to where in the brain it effects along with stories of other cultures think it connects you to.
You can feel that there are more volumes to be added to this series and would be gratefully received by the reading public. I hope he continues this line of work.

Shiva, UK

No, this is not a version of the 1969, multimillion selling Norman Greenbaum song, rather, it is a truly fascinating book that grabs you by the throat and demands to be read. The abundantly illustrated and easy to read work is one of those rare books that forces you to question just about everything you thought you knew. It also makes you say, 'No, surely that can't be right', then you do a double take and ask 'Can it?' This is one of these rare books that has to be read in one sitting then carefully re-read to make sure you fully understood and appreciated the significance of everything that was said. It does this using the psychoactive portal of N-dimethytryptamine (that's DMT to you) to show that reality may well be nothing like we think it is. It also uses certain constellations in the night sky, particularly Orion the Hunter, to show that its image is nigh-on identical to the molecular structure of the aforementioned DMT and apparently the constellation of Canis Major is dead ringer for cannabis as well. This is of course reflected by the iconic Gnostic saying, 'As above, so below', something so remarkably apt that it was hijacked (along with much else that might be useful) by the medieval Catholic Church and repackaged as, 'In heaven as it is on Earth'. The book is subtitled 'Ancient Cosmological Gods & Where in The World We Find Them', and this is something it does remarkably well. Any complaints? Well, it is a bit on the slim side, but other than that the book is alt-history (or maybe alt-reality) at its very, very best and is guaranteed to make even the sceptical reader sit up and ask themselves some serious questions. Highly recommended.

Phenomenia Magazine, UK

Available via Amazon

It's extremely easy to consider our modern society the apex of sophisticated technological evolution. We're somewhat arrogantly striving to conquer outer space with almost zero knowledge of the inner realms of our own spiritual existence. But what if we're not 'the greatest' after all? The Bible's first 3 days of Creation in the book of Genesis are at verses 5, 8 & 13. 5, 8 & 13 are also part of the Fibonacci sequence and the height of the Great Pyramid of Giza once stood at 5,813 inches. A circle with a radius of 5,813 inches, we find, has a circumference of 36,524 inches and there are 365.24 days in a solar year. But when can countless coincidences and correlations be considred as credible and scientifically viable connections? The Ancient Egyptian sun god Amun is symbolically associated with both the sign of the pyramid and the ram, and is also synonymous with Amon, Amen, Jesus, Osiris and Zeus. Amun however, is also acknowledged as Ammon; 'Ammon's Horn' being another name for the hippocampus proper in the human brain which is resposible for higher brain functions such as memory recall. Along with the eyes, lungs, cerebrospinal fluid, the pineal gland and neocortex, Ammon's ram-like horn holds potential to biosynthesise DMT - a highly hallucinogenic chemical compound which may one day be considered a catalyst or indeed key to regulating perceived levels of interdimensional realities. Deities, Myth & Tryptamines uncovers a rich tapestry of archaic appreciation for a biomechanically correct blueprint of the human brain and beyond. The very faberic of this global tradition has been systematically inserted into the zeitgeist of generations of interconnected religions and hidden in plain sight. Ancient art transcends language, and there are many arte-facts to consider...

Reviews

Very intriguing, highly inspiring, intelligent, thought-provoking and eye-opening book. In "Deities, Myth and Tryptamins" R. N. Vooght masterfully arranging the different pieces of the great puzzle into the one coherent and majestic mosaic masterpiece. It becomes obvious, as soon as you have a dip into this amazing book, that the author have done a thorough research into the subject and has a unique vision. R. N. Vooght masterfully connecting dots together, decifering ancient clues left for us in a form of Myths, combining them with the decoded passages from the Bible and pioneering findings of modern science. He impressively combines the elements of Mythology, Bible, Quantum mechanics, Astrology, the mysteries of ancient architecture (such as Karnak temple and great Pyramids), sacred geometry, pineal gland, and "spirit molecule" (DMT) into a truly fascinating "whole". Beautifully illustrated, well researched and written with the sprinkle of gentle humour this amazing book offers a unique and interesting view on the True Nature of Reality. Highly recommend for anyone interested in the decoding of mysteries of Creation.

Shiva, UK

Easy read, with color photos. Your questions answered: what do Egyptian History, the Bible, Many Other Sacred Scriptures, the Cosmos & human mind have in common. You will know this beautiful truth, Feel happier & Empowered, be filled with peace because you will Know Where You Came from & Why You are here. Thank you Universe for showing me the Truth.

Amazon customer, USA

Another absolutely fascinating book by RN Vooght. Thoroughly enjoyed reading about the different theories being explored. Highly recommend this and his first book 'The Spirit in the Sky'. Hoping there may be more to come at some point!

Amazon customer, UK

From the outset it is obvious that the hallucinogen and active ingredient of Ayahuasca dimethyltryptamine (DMT) is seen, by this author at least, as being at the very core of spirituality. And to be fair he is not alone in this assumption. It is also extremely easy to consider our modern society to be at the apex of sophisticated technological evolution and unfortunately, at present our species is fixated on conquering outer-space with almost zero knowledge of the inner realms of our own spiritual existence. Depending on how you look at it, there are signs all around us that things are not as we assume them to be and the proof is all around us and always has been. The author points out that the Bible's first three days of creation in the book of Genesis are in verses 5, 8 and 13. These numbers 5, 8 and 13 are also part of the Fibonacci sequence, and the height of the Great Pyramid of Giza once stood as 5813 inches. A circle with a radius of 5813 inches has a circumference of 36,524 inches and there are 365.24 days in a solar year and there are almost countless examples of thiskind. A coincidence? Maybe! N o doubt the readers of this magazine will have encountered many similar 'facts' from other sources trying to make similar points. This is the second book by the same author where he develops his hypothesis that 'we are not and never have been alone' and the use of DMT (which is naturally present in all human beings) if used wisely will reveal all.

Phenomena Magaine, UK

Fantastic follow up to Spirit in the Sky. I can't even put this into words. Recommend for any truth seeker. Allow yourself to be challenged. Easy read. Near impossible to put down.

St. Krebs, USA

Really enjoyed diving into this book. RN Vooght has some fascinating ideas and makes some really good and interesting connections between some of the world's sacred texts, astrology, and science. The book itself is fairly short, but weaves a really interesting narrative that connects the dots throughout. The view that ancient folklore and mythology should not be taken literally isn't new, but looking at it from the viewpoint that it is deeply entrenched in our ancestors' use of entheogens most definitely is. Well worth picking this title up. Looking forward to reading his other works as well.

Martin, USA

RN Vooght sets the tone in the first part of this book with ancient esoteric symbolism and references to the late great John Anthony West and Schwaller de Lubicz. He does a great job of connecting his own research to the esoteric and mystery traditions will also paying tribute to the great researchers and theories on these topics. I have had the pleasure of interviewing RN on our podcast and it is clear he knows his stuff and has a passion for researching these topics.

Mind Escape Podcast, USA

CONTACT: Myth-illogical@hotmail.com

Twitter: @VooghtRN

Instagram: @RNVooght

Facebook: RN Vooght

Facebook: Deities, Myth & Tryptamines

YouTube Channel: RN Vooght

FURTHER GNOSIS

The Spirit in the Sky, RN Vooght

DMT: Deities, Myth & Tryptamines, RN Vooght

Primal Wisdom of the Ancients, Laird Scranton

The Ancient Language of Sacred Sound, David Elkington

The Missing Lands, Freddy Silva

The Lost Art of Resurrection, Freddy Silva

The Cosmic Serpent, Jeremy Narby

The Spirit Molecule, Rick Strassman

After Skool via YouTube, Mark Wooding

The Jerusalem Stone of Consciousness, Joel David Bakst

YouTube Channel: RN Vooght

Printed in Great Britain
by Amazon